M000210968

"Gloria Furman has a disarming way of connecting the most concrete stuff of our lives to the most glorious truth of the gospel. She's doing it again here, as she peers into the realities of pregnancy and childbirth through the windows of Scripture. This book opens the windows wide. We do well to ponder this theme, of which God keeps reminding us in all kinds of painful and marvelous ways."

Kathleen Nielson, speaker; coeditor, *Word-Filled Women's Ministry* and *Resurrection Life in a World of Suffering*

"Gloria Furman has written devotions that will transform the way we view pregnancy from conception to birth and beyond. *Labor with Hope* magnifies the glory of Christ and all that he has done, and helps us fix our eyes on the one who gives eternal life."

Trillia Newbell, author, *If God Is for Us*; *Fear and Faith*, and *God's Very Good Idea*

"When Gloria Furman speaks about motherhood, I always listen. In *Labor with Hope*, Furman shows us how 'every aspect of childbirth fuels our worship of Jesus,' beautifully unpacking that statement as she takes us on a journey through Scripture, demonstrating how the birth pain metaphor illustrates God's work in us. Each chapter in this meaningful devotional explores a different aspect of this mystery, leading the reader to a fuller understanding of our hope in Christ and the God who labors over us."

Vaneetha Rendall Risner, author, *The Scars That Have Shaped Me: How God Meets Us in Suffering*

"Every part of life belongs to God, even the parts when we're trying to combat the never-ending heartburn, struggling to find that elusive comfortable position, or panting and pushing to birth the long-awaited new addition to God's world. My dear friend (and mother of four) Gloria Furman has crafted beautiful meditations for you to ponder as you labor through your pregnancy and wonder, 'Why is this like it is?' Dear sister, this book will help you understand what's happening and why, and will give you hope for future days of joy in God's good providence. I heartily recommend it!"

Elyse Fitzpatrick, coauthor, *Give Them Grace*

"In stark contrast to many of the childbirth books on shelves today, *Labor with Hope* offers gospel freedom from the burdens and guilt that often surround labor and delivery. With short, easy-to-read devotionals, Gloria Furman unpacks the spiritual realities of childbirth, offering hope and joy to women who pick up this book."

Laura Wifler, Cofounder, Risen Motherhood

"Sin has blurred our vision of motherhood. In this book, Gloria Furman invites us to look through a gospel telescope that helps us focus our blurred, painful, and mundane perspective of pregnancy into a sharp, eternal, and glorious reality."

Betsy Gómez, Blogger, Revive Our Hearts Hispanic Outreach

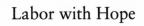

Labor with Hope

GLORIA FURMAN

WITH JESSE SCHEUMANN

Labor with Hope

GOSPEL MEDITATIONS ON PREGNANCY, CHILDBIRTH, AND MOTHERHOOD

CROSSWAY®

WHEATON, ILLINOIS

Labor with Hope: Gospel Meditations on Pregnancy, Childbirth, and Motherhood

Copyright © 2019 by Gloria Furman

Published by Crossway
    1300 Crescent Street
    Wheaton, Illinois 60187

This book is a devotional to encourage your spiritual life. It does not offer medical or health advice regarding fertility, pregnancy, the birthing/labor experience, or the post-birth/labor experience of the mother. Further, this book is not intended to substitute for the advice or care of a physician or medical professional. Readers, especially those with preexisting medical conditions, should always consult a physician or medical professional for any health-related matters or questions.

Cover design: Crystal Courtney

First printing 2019

Printed in the United States of America

Scripture quotations are from the ESV® Bible (The Holy Bible, English Standard Version®), copyright © 2001 by Crossway, a publishing ministry of Good News Publishers. Used by permission. All rights reserved.

All emphases in Scripture quotations have been added by the author.

Hardcover ISBN: 978-1-4335-6307-2
ePub ISBN: 978-1-4335-6310-2
PDF ISBN: 978-1-4335-6308-9
Mobipocket ISBN: 978-1-4335-6309-6

Library of Congress Cataloging-in-Publication Data

Names: Furman, Gloria, 1980– author.
Title: Labor with hope : Gospel meditations on pregnancy, childbirth, and motherhood / Gloria Furman with Jesse Scheumann.
Description: Wheaton : Crossway, 2019. | Includes bibliographical references and index.
Identifiers: LCCN 2018036644 (print) | LCCN 2018054102 (ebook) | ISBN 9781433563089 (pdf) | ISBN 9781433563096 (mobi) | ISBN 9781433563102 (epub) | ISBN 9781433563072 (hc)
Subjects: LCSH: Pregnant women—Religious life. | Pregnancy—Religious aspects—Christianity—Meditations. | Childbirth—Religious aspects—Christianity—Meditations. | Motherhood—Religious aspects—Christianity—Meditations. | Bible—Meditations.
Classification: LCC BV4529.18 (ebook) | LCC BV4529.18 .F864 2019 (print) | DDC 248.8/431—dc23
LC record available at https://lccn.loc.gov/2018036644

Crossway is a publishing ministry of Good News Publishers.

LB		29	28	27	26	25	24	23	22	21	20	19
15	14	13	12	11	10	9	8	7	6	5	4	3	2	1

In his hand is the life of every living thing
and the breath of all mankind.
Job 12:10

To Kim B. and Kris L., heroes of mine whose labor
with hope in the desert is producing fruit beyond
what they could ask or imagine. —G. F.

To my mother, Joyce, who tasted the
curse that I might see life.
To my wife, Merissa, who bore the burden of
childbearing that I might hold our precious babies.
To my children—Rebekah, Peter, and Abigail: may you know
and embrace the sufferings of Christ, being born again. —J. S.

Contents

Acknowledgments

Many people supported me throughout the labor of publishing this book. From the very beginning stages to the end, my husband, Dave, was of great encouragement to me. As I write in the author's note, *Labor with Hope* would not and could not have been written without the expertise of Jesse Scheumann and his wife, Merissa. I'm deeply grateful, as ever, to the team at Crossway for their support of this project and their tireless efforts in spreading the gospel to all nations. Several friends in particular provided the fuel of enthusiasm and prayer over the years: Katie Jennings, Kathleen Nielson, Bev Berrus, Caroline Cobb, Victoria Wilson, and Shelley Reinhart. I'm thankful for Andrew Wolgemuth's consistent encouragement and careful guidance. —*Gloria Furman*

I would like to thank all of the faculty at Bethlehem College and Seminary, who equipped me to read the Bible more carefully and responsibly. I especially thank Jason DeRouchie, who supervised my thesis on birth pain. Your humility, rigor, and godly passion have left an indelible mark. I thank my co-author, Gloria Furman, for penning these theological truths for an audience I never could have reached on my own. Finally, thank you to Crossway for taking on an unexplored topic with an unconventional coauthorship. In all God is preeminent. —*Jesse Scheumann*

Author's Note

Books are like babies in many ways.

Writers often remark on how the work of writing a book carries with it an anticipation and labor that is not dissimilar to that which accompanies pregnancy and birth.

In keeping with this metaphor, it is appropriate to ask how a book was born. You have the conception of an idea for a book, and there's the test to confirm whether or not a publisher will publish it. The writer must wait for a period of time, and eventually a line appears in one's inbox—positive or negative—to announce whether or not there is a book that is going to be born.

Then the real fun (and periodic nausea) begins. Writers labor over their outlines and chapters and sentences and words and punctuation marks. Eventually the writer reaches the end of this literary gestation period and transitions to the stage where one is no longer certain one wants to write a book after all. Enter the literary agent, who cheers for you to "Write! Write!" and reminds you that all of the discomfort is worth it. Sometimes the book is born early, to the editor's delightful surprise, and other times the overdue book must be induced. Either way, at some point an expert editorial team receives your book, cleans it up a bit, wraps it up, and hands it back to you. All the while, the marketing team busily writes book birth announcements, and everyone prays thankful prayers and asks the Lord to make this book a blessing to all who read it.

So, how was *Labor with Hope* born? I had been reading about the birth pain metaphor in Scripture and toying around with the idea of doing my PhD on it so I could have an excuse to research this metaphor even more. And then in 2014 I wrote a brief blog post mentioning some of the passages I noticed in Scripture. A few days later I received an email from someone who read my blog about birth pain because a friend of his sent it to him. Jesse Scheumann said that he had just defended his ThM thesis on the subject at hand, calling it "A Biblical Theology of Birth Pain," and would I like to read a copy of it?

Well, anything that is named "a biblical theology of" sounds interesting already, and this topic in particular? Yes, sir, of course I'd like to read your thesis.

Jesse sent me his thesis along with the encouragement to consider using his academic work to help me write a popular-level book on a biblical theology of birth pain. I took this idea of writing a book seriously because I love the gospel hope in this subject and think it is great fuel for worship. It also has tremendous evangelistic potential for our everyday conversations about Jesus and what he has done.

I thought about this topic off and on for a long time, and though I did not end up starting my PhD, the book idea never went away. All along this journey, Jesse has generously allowed me to use his comprehensive academic work *and* helped tremendously in the architectural phase of the chapter outlines. He spent hours editing what I've written.

And so now, a book is born. I wrote in the original proposal that I thought I could have the manuscript delivered to the publisher within nine months, just to be punny. But like some babies, this one was such a great labor to write that it needed to be induced in the last month.

That the Bible offers meaning and hope in our labor and childbirth does not mean that any preferences for delivery are right or wrong. Nor does our hope in Christ mean that we should dismiss the gift of modern medical care. Please read this book for its intended purpose—as a devotional—and regularly consult your physician for questions about care in pregnancy and childbirth.

I am happy to offer to you *Labor with Hope: Gospel Meditations on Pregnancy, Childbirth, and Motherhood*, and pray that God uses it to point you to his Son, through whom are all things and through whom we exist.

Introduction

Even the midwives were charmed. They don't often witness a birth in which the baby begins to cry before she is fully born. As a volunteer birth doula, this particular scenario was a first for me. Those bleating, newborn cries were music to her mother's ears while she waited for the next big contraction to help birth the baby's shoulders and the rest of her body. The labor had been challenging, and baby's cries helped to give mom the focus and hope she needed to push with everything she had. The big wave came, and as arms reached to catch the baby and the mother's groans turned to laughter, a child was born. Praise God for sustaining life and giving new life!

Chatting about the work they had ahead of them with the laboring woman down the hall, the midwives started to tidy up the delivery room. Traffic hummed and headlights twinkled through the curtains from the busy highway just outside. Meanwhile, the mom and dad were in awe, saying thank you to the Lord and gazing into their daughter's eyes. As she nursed her minutes-old daughter, my friend marveled at God's gentle care: "You'll have the grace you need when you need it." *Amen, sister.* I took an uneventful taxi ride home at two in the morning and crawled into bed. When I woke, my eyes smarted with a tiny fraction of the fresh fatigue the growing family must have been feeling.

Childbirth never gets old. Whether I was the laboring mother with my four children or I am the doula at another mother's side, I weep every time. Childbirth is at the same time a painful trial and a matchless joy, a display of weakness and a feat of strength, a shadow and a reality. Even those who have not given birth can praise God for the fact that our own mothers tasted death in order to give us life. Indeed, God has shown us great mercy.

You may be asking a variety of questions right now—questions regarding the trivial and the concerning as well as the temporary and the eternal. *Is it normal to feel this way? Why are pregnancy and childbirth the way they are? Why is it all so profound? So common? So elusive? So exhausting and scary? So thrilling and hopeful? What will we name the baby? How can two little lines on a pregnancy test evoke our emotions the way they do?*

Just like everything else in life, we want our consideration of pregnancy and birth to be consistent with reality. Sometimes the way we think and feel about pregnancy and birth are more reflections of our misconceptions, cultural values, personal preferences, or even overt lies from the pit of hell. But no one wants to form opinions or make decisions based on false information. We desire to live in the light of truth.

Our bookstores, Internet forums, and colloquial sayings are replete with advice and knowledge for mothers concerning pregnancy and birth. Insofar as they correspond with reality, these resources can be helpful. After all, who doesn't love to see an illustration of how big the baby is in utero as compared to an eggplant? Finding practical tips is like picking up seashells on a beach, but the jewels of wisdom we need for our spiritual well-being can only be mined from God's Word.

Two thousand years ago, Jesus, a man who was born of a virgin (yet is the uncreated Son of God), spoke of himself using these words: "I am the way, and the truth, and the life" (John 14:6). What does this man have to do with how we think about pregnancy and childbirth?

In *Labor with Hope* we will see how Jesus has everything to do with everything, including our spiritual nourishment in pregnancy and childbirth. We will walk together and examine the treasures we find in God's Word concerning many related topics—pregnancy, infertility, miscarriage, birth pain, new physical life—and how these common experiences point us to eternal realities.

At times our pace will be quick, but on some themes we will take our time so you can catch your breath a bit (after all, pregnancy can make one winded!). We'll go back and forth in the Bible's storyline, meditating on the concept of laboring with hope. Worship was my goal in writing this devotional book, and it remains my hope and prayer for readers. "Oh, magnify the LORD with me, and let us exalt his name together!" (Ps. 34:3). Let's marvel together at the God who created life and grants us new life in his Son.

1

In the Image of God
He Created Them

Then God said, "Let us make man in our image, after our likeness. And let them have dominion over the fish of the sea and over the birds of the heavens and over the livestock and over all the earth and over every creeping thing that creeps on the earth."

So God created man in his own image,
　　in the image of God he created him;
　　male and female he created them.

Genesis 1:26–27

"It was a dark and stormy night. Then your mother announced, 'The baby is coming!'" And so begins my own birth story in which my parents had to drive across a bridge to reach the hospital while a snowstorm was brewing (we made it).

Your birth story is no doubt different than mine. After all, the end result of the birth story is *you*, a unique human being. There is a birth story we all share, however. It's the story of the birth of mankind. It starts like this . . .

Once upon a time, before there was time, there was God.

Independent of everything and everyone—God exists. In perfect holiness, diversity, and love, the triune God lives forever.

And then, in the beginning, God created everything you can see and everything you can't see . . . out of nothing. We read the story of creation in Genesis 1. God spoke things into existence: "Let there be . . ." He made the earth, space, time, light, land, and plants. And then he filled it all in—sun, moon, stars, sea and flying creatures, and land animals. It was all good.

Then the Creator did something different. With intimate care and attention, he "formed the man of dust from the ground and breathed into his nostrils the breath of life, and the man became a living creature" (Gen. 2:7). But a helper fit for the man was not found among everything God had made. "So the LORD God caused a deep sleep to fall upon the man, and while he slept took one of his ribs and closed up its place with flesh. And the rib that the LORD God had taken from the man he made into a woman and brought her to the man" (Gen. 2:21–22). When the man awoke and saw her, the man burst into song:

This at last is bone of my bones
    and flesh of my flesh;
she shall be called Woman,
    because she was taken out of Man. (Gen. 2:23)

There they were—two complementary imagers of equal dignity and value—distinctly designed to fit together in unity with a procreative purpose (Mal. 2:15). God saw everything that he had made, and it was *very* good. From the outside in, God created and filled the cosmos, and the epitome of his creative work was his image bearers—man and woman.

A Wonder-Full Thought

Whether you are a brand-new mother or a mother of twelve, it is astonishing that God would grow another one (or more!) of his image bearers in your womb. Though the child is made up of your DNA and bears resemblance to you, he or she is foremost an image bearer of the triune God. As are you.

Pause for a minute to notice the swirling arcs on your fingers. Be conscious of your lungs filling with air, your heart pumping blood through your blood vessels, and your brain controlling your body's functions (even as you sleep). Your life is no accident. Someone is purposefully holding you together (Col. 1:17). Both you and your unborn child belong to the Lord, you are his imagers, and you exist for his glory. As God's imagers we have the unparalleled privilege and responsibility of representing him to the watching cosmos in every capacity he has designed for us.

I know all of this can be hard to understand on a Thursday afternoon. You've got a dozen things on your mind right now, and besides, God is infinite and his ways are above our ways. How can humans think about such things? After all, we are merely physical creatures who are earthbound in our limited comprehension. *But is that all we are?*

Could it be that the Creator of all things had something wonderful in his mind when he made man and woman? Something that shows us how glorious *he* is? God could have charged the six-winged seraphim with representing him to the watching cosmos, yet he fashioned a man out of dust and a woman from the man's rib. Our mammalian lungs could have just simply filled with oxygen like those in the animal realm, yet the Lord chose to breathe into the man his breath of life. Something profound is going on here—something beyond what we can see with the retinas and corneas in our eyes. We would do well to take more time to think about such things, following the dust in the sunbeams up to the sun.

All-You-Can-Eat Truth

Where else can we go to learn about the One for whom we were made but to God's very Word? Through God's gift of medicine, a world of knowledge about fertility, pregnancy, and childbirth is at our disposal to help us nurture both our own bodies and those blooming within our wombs. But when we are looking for spiritual nourishment, we have to dig into the Bible.

And so that's where we will continue to look. The Bible is a buffet with plenty of soul food for those who are eating for two. As the Lord wills, I will use the pages that follow to explain how the entire human experience of childbirth is a signpost for overwhelming joy and realities that will endure forever.

2

Be Fruitful and Multiply

And God blessed them. And God said to them, "Be fruitful and multiply and fill the earth and subdue it, and have dominion over the fish of the sea and over the birds of the heavens and over every living thing that moves on the earth."

Genesis 1:28

"Wouldn't it be so lovely having little versions of you and me running around? I'd love to have a family. *And you think you know what you're talking about . . . you have no idea!*" British comedian Michael McIntyre chided would-be parents during a show. He then described the added complications of mundane life with kids. Through playful humor he made the point that efficiency and comfort do not accompany the task of building a family.[1]

---

1. Michael McIntyre, Christmas Comedy Roadshow, "People with/without Kids," 2011, http://www.michaelmcintyre.co.uk/clips/. (Note: Two instances of mild language used in this clip.)

Perhaps at one level he's right. When it comes to understanding the purpose of having children, we think we know what we're talking about. As confident in our understanding as we may be, we need to ask this question: Where do our ideas about having children come from? We probably would get different answers depending on cultural values, time period, or personal experience.

Little Versions of You and Me Running Around

Because I live in a diverse global city, I get to see many different people groups live out their beliefs in regard to the purpose of having children. Some people aim to have as many children as biologically possible, perhaps with an aim to birthing more boys than girls. Some people embrace the concept of transracial adoption and have grown their family in this way. Some people consciously refrain from having children at all for economic reasons. Some people have more children precisely for economic reasons. Perspectives on fertility are as diverse as the people who hold them. What is the purpose of having little versions of you and me running around? Do we have any idea?

In the Bible, children are considered a blessing because of God's command to "be fruitful and multiply and fill the earth"—known as the "creation mandate." Practically speaking, more kids means more image bearers of God, and more imager bearers of God means the earth will be filled with God's glory. Having children was necessary to fill the earth with little image bearers. On hearing this passage from Scripture, careful readers of the Bible will know this is the way it was in the Old Testament. Careful exegetes of modern cultures will recall scornful nomenclature that reduces women to "baby factories" and controversial practices such as surrogacy and abortion. It is true that in Old Testament times in order to expand and fill the earth with God's glory, God's people focused on biological fertility. But what about now? We live in between the two ages—the one that is passing away and the one that is coming. How do we think about the purpose of having children *now*? Do we need to discard the Bible's teaching at this point? Of course not. Thankfully, the Bible is one book, it is utterly and internally consistent, and it is applicable for all times.

The Old Testament prophet Isaiah pulls back the curtain on how God will ultimately fill the earth with his glory. Isaiah's prophecy concerned an eternal King who would bring about a new humanity through his sufferings. According to the will of God, this Servant would be cut off from this life, crushed, and put to grief, yet he would somehow not only have offspring but he would see them in his prolonged, prosperous life.

> Yet it was the will of the LORD to crush him;
>> he has put him to grief;
> when his soul makes an offering for guilt,
>> he shall see his offspring; he shall prolong his days;
> the will of the LORD shall prosper in his hand. (Isa. 53:10)

This is not humanly possible. Humanly speaking, men who die do not actively bear offspring and see their offspring, nor do they come back to life. It just doesn't happen. But Isaiah isn't describing just *any* man.

How does this Suffering Servant have offspring? And *why*?

From Creation Mandate to the New Creation

There is a man who was, by the will of God, crushed in order to atone for the sin of his offspring. This Man is Jesus, and he sees his offspring every day. He is with them, in fact, to the end of the age, at which point he will dwell with them again and they will see his face. No, Jesus did not have any biological children, but now through his Spirit, his spiritual children are lighting up every dark corner of the globe. Remade into his glorious likeness, men, women, and children who have been given new hearts are filling the earth and making more and more and more disciples of the Servant who suffered for their sake. Let's call this "spiritual fertility"—a kind of procreation that can run circles around our expiring biological clocks.

Starting a family, building a legacy, carrying on the family name . . . do we have any idea what we're talking about? All of these very good things—families, legacies, names—are mere shadows and signposts that hint at something much greater than what we can see with our eyes and measure with a head count at the family reunion. It may be, friend, that you are among those who are not physically able to participate in biological procreation. Be encouraged, because what I am about to say is not a trifling "consolation prize" for you. God's big idea of the way his glory will fill the earth is for all of us to enjoy: "making babies who make more babies" points us to discipleship. The offspring of the Suffering Servant—little versions of Jesus running around—pass on the gospel to those who will pass on the gospel. Our biological and spiritual fertility is facilitated by God for God's glory (not ours). By the power of the Spirit, the new humanity in Christ will fill God's new creation to the praise of his glorious grace. And it will be profoundly more than lovely.

3

The Promised Seed of Woman

I will put enmity between you and the woman,
   and between your offspring and her offspring;
he shall bruise your head,
   and you shall bruise his heel.

Genesis 3:15

Can you imagine life as it was before sin entered the world? Perhaps you can, and that's what intrigues (and perhaps bothers) you.

All creation teemed with life! Proud palm trees lifted their fronds high overhead, and the curious chinchilla darted among the rocks in the mountains. Anglerfish roamed the deep sea with a welcome lantern, and lopsided fiddler crabs shook each other's claws on the beach. Wandering albatross glided aloft wherever the wind took them, and the fragile dove was not yet said to be a "mourning" dove. Everything was good in God's creation.

And then God made something—two *someones*—actually, whom he said were *very* good. Adam and Eve did not know what it felt like to have that nagging suspicion that the other was upset with them. No anxious questions of "what shall we eat, what shall we drink, what shall we wear" came into their minds. God had given them the esteemed privilege of ruling and subduing his creation, along with the capacity to do it for his glory alone. The man and woman were, after all, created in God's image. They were free—free to love God with all their heart, soul, mind, and strength.

God speaks and mankind lives; that is reality. Adam and Eve were to live by every word that proceeded from the mouth of God, and they could eat of every tree in the garden except for one—the tree of the knowledge of good and evil. No distance separated them from God. No bitter feelings moved them to give God the silent treatment. No anger seethed in their hearts because there was nothing to be afraid of. No shameful memories crept into their minds to steal their awareness of the dignity God had given them. No guilty conscience locked their feet in place to prevent them from walking with him every day.

The End of the Beginning

But all of that changed. Adam allowed God's enemy (embodied in a crafty serpent) to hiss doubt into his wife's ears—doubts about who God is and what his heart is like. Adam allowed this deceiver to linger in God's perfect garden, where no unclean thing dwelled.

> Did God actually say, "You shall not eat of any tree in the garden"? (Gen. 3:1)

> You will not surely die. For God knows that when you eat of it your eyes will be opened, and you will be like God, knowing good and evil. (Gen. 3:4–5)

The doubt of all doubts goes like this: perhaps there is a word that is better than God's.

Isn't it ironic? *Disobey* God in order to know good and evil? God's image bearers disbelieved him, and they believed his enemy instead. When they rejected God's Word, they chose to live not by God's words but by his enemy's. They ate the fruit that God forbade them to eat, and as a result they fell into sin, taking all of their children with them. The fracturing of the cosmos on the fault line of human sin cannot be described too strongly. God's image bearers . . . *his* image bearers . . . committed cosmic treason. Instead of discerning that the vile serpent should be judged for entering God's holy place, Adam willfully defected to the other side. He laid aside the priestly, kingly, and prophetic authority given to him by his Creator, and found himself and his offspring—not to mention the rest of creation—careening into the abyss of sin, death, and judgment.

No amount of "I'm really sorry's" can atone for such treachery. No quantity of good works can be done to make up for what was lost. No amount of whitewash can cover up the stain of sin that now saturated the human heart.

The Hope of All Humanity

God would have been perfectly just to not allow Adam and Eve to live for even a single second after they sinned against him in the garden. Unless God himself intervenes on our behalf, all is lost forever.

What did God do? He promised he would send a Deliverer. A Promised One would come, leading the way of rebellion against the fallen world order of sin. A terrible battle for the eternal souls of men would ensue, and God's Promised One would emerge victorious. As he indicted his enemy, God made the announcement that flips everything right side up again:

I will put enmity between you and the woman,
>   and between your offspring and her offspring;
he shall bruise your head,
>   and you shall bruise his heel. (Gen. 3:15)

Did you catch that? God said the woman would have off-spring—a singular, male offspring. "He" would bruise the head of Satan (a mortal wound), yet "his heel" would be wounded (a comparatively minor wound). The hope of human history hangs on the promise that a Deliverer would come through the woman's womb. God kept his promise. Jesus—the last Adam—prevailed over God's enemy and is now putting the cosmos back in its rightful order.

God did not annihilate us in the garden. Before God spoke a word of judgment to Adam and Eve, he gave them this word of life. Childbirth—new physical life—is evidence of God's ongoing mercy to sinful humanity. Everyone who has ever been born has tasted this mercy. After the fall, when death entered into God's creation, every soul conceived is a triumph of life despite death. The fact of life reminds us that we have Jesus, and if we have Jesus then we have hope.

4

Why Does Childbirth Hurt So Bad?

To the woman he said,

"I will surely multiply your pain in childbearing;
    in pain you shall bring forth children.
Your desire shall be contrary to your husband,
    but he shall rule over you."

Genesis 3:16

A friend of mine once said that because he had stepped on a Lego block with his bare foot, he now knew what childbirth felt like. Of course, he was only joking, but in all seriousness, why does birth pain hurt so much?

"Why? *Why* all this pain?" a laboring woman sobbed in my arms in a delivery room. Various world religions propose different explanations. What do you believe is the answer? Do you think birth pain exists just for physiological reasons? Or is there something more to it? What do your neighbors think about this common human experience? It would make for an interesting conversation to ask your friends what they believe to be the origin of birth pain and if they think it serves a metaphysical purpose.

Even the scientific community has attempted to quantify the physical pain experienced by women in labor.[1] Such a task proves to be elusive, as pain is experienced in many other capacities—it's not just physical. Can you measure the emotional toll of the past nine months (combined with present circumstances in the delivery room), the mental distress that "this is really happening," and the often alarming capacity for spiritual uneasiness when the contractions are coming too slowly (or quickly)? How do you explain the reason why many women who do not acknowledge God (or any "god") in their everyday lives suddenly cry out to a higher power when they are in the throes of labor? Who can comprehend the culmination of all manner of pain when it is time to push? And how does one summarize the tidal wave of different emotions that swell when you leave the delivery room and live through the joy-mingled pain of raising children?

If what C. S. Lewis says is right—that pain is God's "megaphone to rouse a deaf world"[2]—then women experiencing birth pain might be the most spiritually attentive people in the world.

Where Did This Megaphone Come From?

We read in the Bible that God had commissioned Adam and Eve to be fruitful and multiply, but in judgment for their sin God said he would now "multiply pain" in being fruitful. It's a play

---

1. Julie Bonapace et al., "No. 355—Physiologic Basis of Pain in Labour and Delivery: An Evidence-Based Approach to Its Management," *Journal of Obstetrics and Gynaecology Canada* 40, no. 2 (2018): 227–45.
2. C. S. Lewis, *The Problem of Pain* (1940; New York: HarperCollins,1996), 91. "God whispers to us in our pleasures, speaks in our conscience, but shouts in our pain: it is His megaphone to rouse a deaf world."

on words in the original Hebrew language. God told Eve her pain would be multiplied in her multiplying. The curse affects childbearing beyond the womb.

To the woman he said,

> "I will surely multiply your pain in childbearing;
> in pain you shall bring forth children.
> Your desire shall be contrary to your husband,
> but he shall rule over you." (Gen. 3:16)

We recall that Eve, created in God's image, had been given an extraordinary role to play as she and Adam were told to "be fruitful and multiply and fill the earth and subdue it" (Gen. 1:28). This particular judgment directly frustrated Eve's procreative capacities, hindering her from easily carrying out God's creation mandate. And now today—all over the world—women in different seasons of life experience hormonal imbalances, fertility issues, miscarriages, pregnancy complications, menstrual pain, stillbirth, menopause, and maternal death. We can only imagine Eve's prefall aptitude for childbearing.

Because we see in God's Word that birth pain is a particular aspect of judgment for our sin, we understand that a woman's labor pain is unlike that of amoral animals. When human beings are delivered through pregnancy and birth pain, there is more going on than biological processes and physiological mechanics. Our multiplied pain in multiplying is intended to point us to a profound theological reality: we need a Deliverer. We will see later in this book how our Deliverer also experienced pain in his labor of multiplying. But before we get too far ahead of ourselves . . .

Can You Hear Hope?

At time of this writing, approximately 7.6 billion souls are dwelling on this earth. One hundred percent of us were born through or despite the existence of birth pain (including those of us who were conceived or born via surgical interventions that were developed to counteract the obstacles we face in reproduction). All mothers and babies who are delivered through pregnancy and labor are recipients of God's undeserved common grace, which includes all of us. Corporately we have plenty of reason to praise God at all times in every way. On this corporate level—as those who have been delivered by the grace of God—we can reflect on birth pain and see a distinct picture of our plight as sinful, rebellious creatures. Oh, how we need someone to deliver us! We are helpless to save ourselves.

Personally, individually, we hear through the megaphone of birth pain a call to repentance and faith in Christ. Can you hear it? As he hung dying on the cross, despised and rejected by God and men, Jesus travailed under the just wrath of God for our sin. Jesus willingly did this in our place as our substitute—he is *the* Lamb of God. A glorious transaction was made on that cross: Jesus purchased redemption for his offspring. What a costly hope we have in Christ, who paid for our salvation with his blood.

It ought to be explicitly said now: No mother can make atonement for herself (or anyone else) in the birthing room. Only the blood of Jesus could satisfy the wrath of God against our sin. There is no merit achieved by undergoing a painful labor (neither is there merit lost through receiving pain-relieving medication). Our labor pain has a divine origin and significance, but we serve a God of mercy (Ex. 34:6); he does not demand that we suffer through it without help.

In our place condemned for our sin, Jesus's pain was multiplied in his multiplying. Jesus satisfied the wrath of God at the cross, and by his blood he ransomed people for God from every tribe and language and people and nation (Rev. 5:9). And now everyone who is a believer in Jesus Christ—whether male or female, child or adult—can hear through the megaphone of birth pain that God's righteous judgment for our sin was borne on the cross by his sinless Son. The Bible says that when Jesus's travails on the cross had reached their end, he declared, "It is finished" (John 19:30).

5

Pain in Parenting

> Now Adam knew Eve his wife, and she conceived and bore Cain, saying, "I have gotten a man with the help of the LORD." And again, she bore his brother Abel. Now Abel was a keeper of sheep, and Cain a worker of the ground. . . . Cain spoke to Abel his brother. And when they were in the field, Cain rose up against his brother Abel and killed him.
>
> *Genesis 4:1–2, 8*

"How are your kids?" It's an easy question to ask in casual conversation, one I find myself asking others all the time. But this is a tricky question to answer. It makes mothers pause. Maternal pride in a mother's heart swells when she thinks of her kids. Concurrently, a variety of anxieties may be trying to get her attention. This question could also wedge open the crack in the weakening wall of the levee, letting loose an overwhelming flood of grief.

In a casual conversation a mother can easily answer the question with the general reply, "Good!" but she can always think of a thousand different things she could say.

You would not have to think for very long to come up with a list of the mothers in your life who are living with a broken heart because of the pain in their parenting. An intensity matched only by her fierce love for her children, a mother's agony may swell and burst like waves crashing.

Because we live in a fallen world, suffering is reality. This pain is part of the curse. The judgment of Genesis 3:16 addresses the physical pain of childbirth specifically (from puberty to menopause!). But we also see empirical evidence of how sin, judgment, and suffering impact all areas of motherhood generally. The pain of pregnancy and birth are both a preparation and precursor for the trials ahead.

You may know people who have observed these various parenting pains and then chosen not to bring children into "a world like this one." Mothers (and fathers) watch their children suffer, and suffer with them. Many mothers suffer greatly for their children, or even suffer because of them. Some mothers witness their children inflict pain—on themselves, on others, and even on the mother who bore them. It is devastating to consider the reality of our brokenness as human beings. Across the globe and throughout history, a mother's experience is diverse and wide-ranging, from the socially acceptable lament of "my kids are making me crazy" to the unspeakable griefs that a mother would never dare to utter aloud. Along the lines of Lewis's comment on pain rousing a deaf world to the existence of God, the megaphone of maternal pain calls us to repent and believe in the gospel—the one resolution to our sorrow. While the pain of pushing may last mere hours or minutes, the pain of parenting in this sin-sick world can last a lifetime. At every point in this journey of parenting, we mother our children by grace through faith in Jesus.

God Help Us

My circle of friends and acquaintances in this global city represent only a minuscule fraction of the diversity present in the world today. But among these women, we share many commonalities with one another. One is that the effects of judgment for our sin reach far past our wombs. We all need hope and help for our labors in parenting. We need to know there is a resolution to our suffering. We all need to see how our pain as mothers points us to a man who hung on a cross for our sin and three days later walked out of his grave for our justification.

In the first few verses of Genesis 4 we read that Eve became pregnant, persevered through pregnancy, and survived childbirth—twice! The Lord delivered Eve through her increased pain in multiplying. She explicitly acknowledges that God is the one who is responsible for her successful conception, childbirth, and deliverance. She calls him by his personal, covenant name—"the LORD." Eve gives credit where it is due. I'm filled with hope when I consider that whereas Eve had been in error in her representation of God while speaking with the evil serpent, here she has no doubt whatsoever in God's trustworthy and gracious character.

Our covenant-making, promise-keeping God had said that a serpent-crushing man—the Messiah—would come through the seed of the woman. And now Eve recognizes that she has "gotten a man with the help of the LORD." What a thrill! Mothers who have persevered through pregnancy and labor in order to hold a squalling infant in their arms—no matter how long ago it was—can still taste the trembling joy of that moment. For Eve, this moment meant much more than simply being given a baby to love and to raise in the fear of the Lord. Her and Cain's deliverance through labor were a signal to her that God's promises would endure. Perhaps Eve examined Cain and Abel's chubby little feet and their tiny toenails wondering how a son of hers would one day crush the head of the vile serpent.

Eve's dreams of deliverance through Cain and Abel were crushed, however, when it was revealed that Cain was no match for the serpent. Cain, filled with hate, murdered his brother. In one blow, the mother of all living lost both of her sons. One of her sons was slain and the other was revealed to be on the serpent's side and was not her promised Deliverer. Who would deliver them now? God had provided for her in the daily trials she faced as a mom raising kids with a sinful nature in a broken habitat outside of God's perfect garden. Was this all for naught? What went wrong? Why such overwhelming heartache?

Hope Like Eve

Perhaps this question—*Why?*—haunts you, too. Perhaps you rehearse a litany of your sacrificial, motherly service and love and conclude: I carried her, I raised her, I fed her and clothed her, so why this pain? What hope can I have?

Adam and Eve's sin, our sin, and the sins of all humanity deserve the righteous judgment of our holy God. God does not err in his judgment. "The Rock, his work is perfect, for all his ways are justice. A God of faithfulness and without iniquity, just and upright is he" (Deut. 32:4). Considering the utter holiness of God should humble us sinners low.

Our pain is greatly multiplied. Dear readers, we all suffer. Like Eve, we cannot assume we will be given conception. Like Eve, we cannot presume that we (or our children) will persevere through pregnancy or that we (and our children) will be delivered through labor pains. Like Eve, we cannot assume our children will "turn out" the way we hope.

It is a hard truth to accept, but a solid one to stand on: we cannot deliver ourselves. May God's rich kindness to us lead us to repentance. Like Eve, we can trust God to keep his promise.

Only the grace of God through Jesus Christ can deliver us from the worst pain and fate a human being can endure—eternal separation from God and punishment in hell. Now, since God has provided deliverance from this fate worse than death, will he not also provide deliverance from our doubts in his character, from our faithlessness as we go on autopilot and forget him, from our arrogant, stubborn hearts that insist we can save ourselves and our children?

May God's faithfulness be what gets us out of bed in the morning, closes our eyes at night, and sustains us during the nights filled with mothering work. Like Eve, let us give credit where it is due, praise God for the various means of common grace in our lives like the medical community, and cling to the Lord who has saved us by grace through faith.

6

Writhing under God's Judgment

You have led in your steadfast love the people whom you
    have redeemed;
   you have guided them by your strength to your holy abode.
The peoples have heard; they tremble;
   pangs have seized the inhabitants of Philistia.
Now are the chiefs of Edom dismayed;
   trembling seizes the leaders of Moab;
all the inhabitants of Canaan have melted away.
   Terror and dread fall upon them;
because of the greatness of your arm, they are still as a stone,
   till your people, O LORD, pass by,
till the people pass by whom you have purchased.

Exodus 15:13–16

These past few chapters haven't been feel-good chapters,
have they? Sin, pain, curse, death, judgment.

We don't often speak of these things in line at the grocery
store or when we pass by a colleague's office. It isn't that these

issues are not real, but that they are acutely, verifiably real and horrifying, and so we'd rather avoid them. Many people are quite comfortable speaking about their health or financial problems in detail. Readers who are currently pregnant, have you confided in a friend or stranger about any new physical ailments? Mothers pursuing adoption, do you find camaraderie with others over the various stresses of adoption? When people share their health struggles or concerns with money or fear of the future or any other specific trial, it rightly solicits our empathy and concern. God designed us to find comfort in community, and we thank him directly for providing shoulders we can cry on and medical professionals who will walk with us through these various types of pain.

But although we might discuss our temporal, physical pains, most of us prefer not to dive with others into the deeper waters of sin and God's judgment. In our hesitation to enter into these discussions together, we miss out. When we gloss over the hard things, we neglect the beauty of God's perfect character. Thankfully the Bible invites us to see our King in all his beauty, as Scripture speaks often of these hard matters in plain, narrative language and even in song, as we see here in Exodus.

Singing with Moses

We have already touched on the fact that both the pain we experience in childbirth *specifically* and the pain we experience in mothering *generally* is part of the curse. We recognize that Adam and Eve's sin, our sin, and the sin of all humanity deserve God's righteous judgment. From birth to death we have pain. If we have ears to hear spiritual things, then we understand how our pain can serve us like an alarm bell or a megaphone. Pain beckons us to live in humble repentance and confident faith in

Christ. Here in Exodus 15 the language of birth pain once again invites us to worship our holy God.

The context of the song in Exodus 15 is deliverance. Safe and sound on the other side of the Red Sea, Moses is teaching the newly rescued people of God to worship their Creator, who has revealed to them his name—Yahweh—which means "I am who I am." Through poetic parallelism, we read about how God, who, by the blasting wind [*ruah*, often translated "Spirit"] of his nostrils, piled up waters and placed his chosen people on dry land (Ex. 15:8). This takes place at the end of the cosmic battle between Yahweh and his enemies in Egypt—both seen and unseen—and Moses's song is like the final ballad in a movie soundtrack while the credits are rolling.

Moses's song is set to the tune of God's faithfulness to his holy name. God is faithful and holy in his deliverance of his people; God is faithful and holy to destroy his enemies. And now, over in the Promised Land, the Canaanites are described as metaphorically writhing in dreadful anticipation of the wrath of God that is coming their way. Their writhing will not lead to their birth and life, but is a sign of their death and destruction. It's important to know that the use of birth pain language to describe judgment is not unique to the Canaanites; it is also used elsewhere in Scripture. A few examples include:

> This day I will begin to put the dread and fear of you on the peoples who are under the whole heaven, who shall hear the report of you and shall tremble and be in anguish because of you. (Deut. 2:25)

> For I heard a cry as of a woman in labor,
> anguish as of one giving birth to her first child,
> the cry of the daughter of Zion gasping for breath,

> stretching out her hands,
> "Woe is me! I am fainting before murderers." (Jer. 4:31)

> Therefore my loins are filled with anguish;
>> pangs have seized me,
>> like the pangs of a woman in labor;
> I am bowed down so that I cannot hear;
>> I am dismayed so that I cannot see. (Isa. 21:3)

No anesthesia on earth can relieve this kind of suffering. Judgment means that, apart from Christ, sin is ours to suffer for eternity.

From Writhing to Rescue

"See now that I, even I, am he, and there is no god beside me; I kill and I make alive; I wound and I heal; and there is none that can deliver out of my hand" (Deut. 32:39). Oh friend, you and I have no moral high ground to stand on in the face of God's righteousness. It is tempting to read this passage and exclusively identify with the delivered ones who are singing the victory song. Remember often that *apart from Christ*, we are the Philistines who are seized with pangs of horror at the notion of God's coming wrath. But for the gospel, we are the Edomites who are dismayed without hope. Without the crucifixion of the Son of God in our place, we are the Moabite leaders who have no good news to offer our families. Never forget that terror and dread and melting away are all rightly ours to have to their fullest measure, if Christ did not drink the full cup of God's wrath for us.

We must embrace the way of deliverance that God has accomplished for us with his own hand. Our throes of agony for fear of God's wrath will not be abated if we are not covered in the blood of Jesus Christ, our Passover Lamb. Jesus was pierced for our transgressions. Jesus was crushed for our iniquities. Upon Jesus was the chastisement that brought us peace, and with Jesus's wounds we are healed.

It is Yahweh himself who guides us to his dwelling place by his strength alone; we cannot accomplish this deliverance for ourselves. If we do not have Jesus, then we cannot expect rescue from God but only his righteous judgment for our sin.

Friend, do you know the comfort of the cross today? When your heart quakes with dread because of your sin, think of Christ who writhed in agony on the cross under the weight of your sin. Do you feel trapped in your sin? Remember how he accomplished the greatest exodus for us from death to new creation life. Let those of us who are proud recall the suffering of Christ in our place, and may it humble our hearts even now. Sing with Moses and marvel at the astonishing holiness of the God who loves us and redeemed us at such a great cost to himself.

7

God's Birth Pain

So Moses cried to the LORD, "What shall I do with this people? They are almost ready to stone me." And the LORD said to Moses, "Pass on before the people, taking with you some of the elders of Israel, and take in your hand the staff with which you struck the Nile, and go. Behold, I will stand before you there on the rock at Horeb, and you shall strike the rock, and water shall come out of it, and the people will drink." And Moses did so, in the sight of the elders of Israel. And he called the name of the place Massah and Meribah, because of the quarreling of the people of Israel, and because they tested the LORD by saying, "Is the LORD among us or not?"

Exodus 17:4–7

In the previous chapter we read how anguish like birth pain has gripped the idolatrous nations in Canaan by the heart and won't let go. Why? Because while Yahweh saved his people, he also punished the Egyptians for their sin, and the Canaanites were next. Throughout the Old Testament, the predominant use of the birth pain metaphor is to indicate the Lord's righteous judgment against sin. The world with all her technology and philosophies cannot rescind his resolution to punish sin or relieve our trembling hearts in the face of what is coming. The nations were right to writhe.

So now that her enemies in the land are quaking in dreadful anticipation, does Israel fearlessly trust the God who saved them from Egypt and led them through the Red Sea? Hardly. Complaining commences, and the people basically initiate a lawsuit against Moses because they are thirsty. Moses recognizes that their grumbling was not really about him: "Why do you quarrel with me? Why do you test the LORD?" The passage above is the LORD's astonishing response to the peoples' rebellious hearts. Read it again slowly. What is happening here?

Indignant in their sin, the Israelites irrationally accuse Yahweh of leading them out of Egypt in order to destroy them. Our sin makes us think ridiculous thoughts, doesn't it? But what does this righteous and holy God do? By his perfect nature and for the sake of his name he cannot tolerate sin. There at Meribah Yahweh stood on the rock and received the judgment blow for the people in their place, and life-giving water flowed from the rock. Instead of striking out at the people in their sin, God (who never does anything wrong) takes the judgment on himself. Does this remind you of something? Keep reading.

Glimpses of Grace at the Rock

Later on, God gave Moses a final song to teach the people after they sojourned in the wilderness and were about to cross into the Promised Land. A line in the song uses the language of birth pain: "You were unmindful of the Rock that bore you, and you forgot the God who gave you birth [through anguish]" (Deut.

32:18). In the last chapter we looked at Deuteronomy 2:25, which said that the nations were in the "anguish" of birth pain. Moses uses the related Hebrew verb here to talk about God birthing his covenant people. How remarkable that he did so by experiencing anguish! What could that refer to?

It may seem strange to think about God experiencing birth pain. God, through the prophet Isaiah, will later say of his salvific work, "I will cry out like a woman in labor; I will gasp and pant" (Isa. 42:14). Gasping and panting are responses to the hard work of labor. We recall that birth pain is largely negative in the Old Testament as it concerns judgment. But do you see how in Deuteronomy 32:18 it is paired with hope? This song was given as a witness and warning, and yet the heartbeat behind it is hope! Again, the metaphor of childbirth points us to God—birth is not about us.

Can you see this breathtaking picture of substitutionary atonement? Look through the lens of the cross, and the fuzzy pixels suddenly sharpen into focus and we catch a glimpse of the glorious gospel. Wicked sinners reject their Savior. They're not asking for mercy. They're shaking their fists. Yet our loving, holy God receives the judgment blow in their place. And the result? God's people are born.

Oh, how we need eyes to see that God is the center of the universe! As dizzying as the pain we experience in raising children can be, we need to have the wherewithal to remember how it points us to God himself. Our fertility complications are not about us. Our pregnancy pains are not about us. Our labor in building our family is not about us. In eternity past the triune God ordained that the crucifixion of the Son of God would be the means of our salvation. *Prior* to Creation. *Prior* to Adam and Eve's sin in the garden. *Prior* to his pronouncement of the judgment of multiplied pain in childbirth. *Prior* to the rock incident at Meribah. All along, God designed the just judgment for our sin to exemplify his lavish grace. Do you see it?

God Is Not Like Us; We Are Like Him

We need to have eyes to see how even the judgment of multiplied pain in childbirth—this common experience of women all over the world throughout the centuries—serves to redirect our thoughts to Jesus. Do not be unaware, sisters . . . the Rock was Christ (1 Cor. 10:1–4). We need to see that our birth pain is like God's, not the other way around. Our birth pain in bringing new life into the world corresponds to God's birth pain in bringing his covenant people into new creation life. We labor with hope as those on whom the end of the ages has come (1 Cor. 10:11).

Lest anyone misunderstand, our birth pain doesn't purify us. The blood of Christ purifies us. We who embrace the gospel believe that nothing can add to Christ's atoning work. Experiencing the judgment of multiplied pain in childbirth cannot assuage a guilty conscience. Making sacrifices in our motherhood cannot cleanse us from our sin. Pretending we are able to deliver ourselves from our sin cannot confirm our dignity as women or mothers. We can't do these things for ourselves, and we don't need to. One time and only one time did Jesus offer himself as a sacrifice for the sins of many, and not a single one of our sins was left uncovered by his blood. We boast in the cross where Christ took the judgment blow for us.

Our Motherhood Is about a Man: Jesus

God delivers those who could never help themselves. The incident at the Rock where God receives the judgment blow in order to give life to his people points us to Christ's suffering on the cross to give new creation life to his people. It is through his suffering that we are born again; you and I didn't do anything except be sinners in need of a Savior. Ours is a daily call to humble, repentant, and grateful mothering laborers.

Let's be broken over our sin. Let's be bold before God's throne of grace. Let's be needy to hear from God's Word every day.

What a relief to learn that our birth pain and motherhood is ultimately not about us, and that it serves to point us to our only hope. Be mindful of the Rock that bore you. Remember the God who gave you birth. Christ is all.

8

The Gospel Is the Ultimate Cure for the Abortion Epidemic

You were unmindful of the Rock that bore you,
  and you forgot the God who gave you birth.

Deuteronomy 32:18

Greater love has no one than this, that someone lay down his life for his friends.

John 15:13

Friend, it took me many attempts to sit down and write this chapter. I would sit down with my laptop open and just weep. One weeping spell in particular lasted on and off all day. The grief was so great that I considered deleting this chapter from the table of contents entirely. But God is kind, and I beheld his love for me at the cross where Jesus bore the penalty for my years of apathy and disregard for human life, because in my youth I considered abortion to be a "sad, but necessary choice" if I were ever to become pregnant before I felt I was ready. I commended friends who aborted their babies, thinking they "did what they had to do" and deliberately closed my eyes to the truth of what abortion is—an assault on the image of God.

When I became a Christian, I repented of this sinful attitude, and on the occasion of writing this book the Spirit has once again comforted my conscience that my guilt is paid for on the cross. And so wherever you are coming from—and from whatever place you are reading this book right now—please read and consider these things where I have considered them: at the foot of the cross of Jesus Christ. And if abortion is part of your story in any capacity, there is no better place for us to consider such a weighty topic than in view of the Savior who has atoned for every sin of every person who places her faith in him.

God's Purposeful Patience

As we saw in the last chapter, our sin makes us think ridiculous thoughts. We act on our maligned beliefs, feelings of hopeless desperation, and even our ignorance. Praise God that he is long-suffering in his patience.

Now, one can exercise long-suffering patience with different intentions. We can all think of people who have waited for the right moment for ill intent, whether they waited to make a snide comment or to take revenge. But the Bible teaches that God's intention in his long-suffering patience is for our repentance: "The Lord is not slow to fulfill his promise as some count slowness, but is patient toward you, not wishing that any should perish, but that all should reach repentance" (2 Pet. 3:9).

What is this promise? "The day of the Lord" is the promise in view here—the promise that Christ will return. Peter tells his readers that God isn't slow. He's deliberately giving us time and opportunity to trust Christ, repent of our sin, and live by faith. Friend, if you woke up this morning (and I can safely assume that you did), then God is showing you his mercy. If you are in Christ, you get to glory in the gospel even now—what a blessing! If you do not know the Lord, he is giving you time right now so that you may yet repent and believe in Christ crucified in your place.

How Long, O Lord?

God's patience is a grace to us, which is particularly striking in light of the grievous sin of abortion. A tide of innocent blood sweeps over the globe and cries out from the earth. When we look at the statistics of abortions across the world, our hearts stagger. So many of us close our eyes to the truth, and so many of us are content with callous layers of apathy on our hearts. So many of us feel utterly hopeless, to the point that we neglect to pray.

We marvel at the Lord's extraordinary, grace-full patience and worship him. He is the epitome of patient love. Recall how Yahweh delivered the Israelites from Egypt. With plagues of blood-rivers, lice, frogs, hail, and the angel of death, he punished the Egyptians for their sin, but from all of these judgments he spared the Israelites. When all of that was said and done, it was through doorways covered in the blood of the Passover Lamb and through walls of water at the Red Sea that Yahweh led the children of Abraham to safety. One would assume that such mercy on God's part in drawing them out of slavery would draw out of their hearts a never-ending current of gratitude. But the human heart is poisoned with corruption. When faced with a trial at the rock of Meribah, the people failed the test . . . miserably. Instead of praise and prayer, complaining and spite flowed out of their hearts.

By his perfect nature and for the sake of his holy name, God cannot tolerate sin. So what would he do? Long-suffering in his patience, not willing that any should perish, Yahweh stood before the rock and received the judgment blow for the people in their place. As God symbolically received the just punishment for the people's sin, life-giving water gushed out of the rock. There at the rock of Meribah, Yahweh gave birth to his people. Sin was judged, and new life was given.

His Life for Ours

"You were unmindful of the Rock that bore you, and you forgot the God who gave you birth." This song was to be on the lips of God's people and echoing in their hearts as a witness and a warning. Don't forget God! Don't *ever* forget God!

Yahweh's willing self-sacrifice for sinners should give us pause. Who are we that he would love us? Who are we that he would pour out his grace upon grace? The answer is not that we are lovely, but that God is love. He is God; he defines love. When we love, we are to love like he loves; he isn't constrained to love us in the way we define love. Praise God for that!

This is why arguments for abortion are diametrically opposed to the heart of the gospel. Yahweh could have struck down the nation of Israel or "aborted" Israel there at the rock, destroying the people with just judgment. Instead, God symbolically received the judgment they deserved in an act that foreshadowed the redemption we receive through the cross, where the God-man experienced death so that we might experience new life.

We gasp and cover our mouths with our hands at the number of abortions committed in our day. It hits close to home for many of us personally. Those numbers represent *our* babies, *our* nephews and nieces, *our* friends and neighbors' children—gone.

Our hearts are heavy, burdened by despair, guilt, and hopelessness. But the gospel gives life and hope! Jesus has borne the guilt of every abortion committed by those whose hope is in him.

Jesus was cut off from his Father on the cross so he could give life to those who have cut off children from life. Jesus writhed under the birth pangs of judgment to remove the blood-guilt of people who have taken life. For the joy set before him, Jesus willingly paid the price to bear spiritual children and redeem them out of this wicked world. Abortion perverts both mercy and justice by means of child sacrifice: your life for mine. But the self-sacrifice of Jesus exemplifies both mercy and justice perfectly: *my life for theirs.*

It should not surprise us that when our culture rejects the gospel, men and women blind themselves and try to escape suffering and sacrifice. In motherhood, a woman mimics the grand narrative of redemption, as she tastes a thousand deaths to give the child life day in and day out. The heartbeat of a birth mother's sacrifice and emotional journey after she has borne a child for adoption is *my life for his.* It is the grace and mercy of God that carries a birth mother through this kind of self-sacrifice and suffering. Jesus said and showed that "greater love has no one than this, that someone lay down his life for his friends" (John 15:13).

Only the message of the gospel offers forgiveness for abortion. Only the gospel is able to empower sacrificial love when we're faced with the choice to take life or nurture it. Only the gospel can reverse the course of the rising number of abortions in our lands.

9

Tasting Death for Others

Yet it was the will of the LORD to crush him;
    he has put him to grief;
when his soul makes an offering for guilt,
    he shall see his offspring; he shall prolong his days;
the will of the LORD shall prosper in his hand.

Isaiah 53:10

But we see him who for a little while was made lower than the angels, namely Jesus, crowned with glory and honor because of the suffering of death, so that by the grace of God he might taste death for everyone. For it was fitting that he, for whom and by whom all things exist, in bringing many sons to glory, should make the founder of their salvation perfect through suffering.

Hebrews 2:9–10

Becoming a mother is an exercise in hyper self-awareness. Think about it: Is there any aspect of your life that is *not* closely scrutinized through the lens of impending motherhood? You're suddenly counting kicks, counting your pounds and the baby's ounces, or counting money for adoption agency fees. You're evaluating your folic acid intake, your closet space, your thermostat, and your car's seating capacity. Even the people around you revert your attention back to yourself through their verbal commentary. *You should eat this. Don't carry that. Buy this. Take this class. How many more months until you bring your son home? Look at your belly—it's so big. Look at your belly—it's so small.* (As if you hadn't already glanced at the calendar or mirror multiple times already that day.) This hyper self-awareness doesn't pack up and leave after forty weeks; it nudges the door open for loneliness.

Isn't it sad how sympathetic comments from other moms about motherhood have the potential to lay more bricks on the wall that isolates us from others? Seemingly safe inside the wall of loneliness, there's no one who completely understands everything we're going through as we die to ourselves to bring life into the world.

Friend, you know I'm going to say, *Yes, there is someone, with all his heart—it's Jesus!* But how can Jesus—a man who was never pregnant and mailed no adoption dossiers to any embassies— know what it's like? I think you'll find that the anchor of hope holds stronger and stronger when we dive deeper into the reasons why Jesus is uniquely empathetic to us, making him exclusively qualified to lead us through suffering into glory.

Following Our Elder Brother

The short answer to our question is: because Jesus himself suffered. The passages above tell what he went through, why he went through it, and the results. It makes all the difference to our perspective on motherhood that we are as aware or "omniconscious" as we can be of our Savior, Jesus.

No doubt you're noticing a pattern: every aspect of motherhood serves to fuel our worship of Jesus. We take our eyes off of ourselves and look through the shadows to the substance, who is Christ. Birth is not about us, but about God.

In view of the watching cosmos, our High Priest Jesus gave himself as a once-and-for-all sacrifice to make us complete. This gave us (men and women and children) unprecedented access to God's presence in the true Holy of Holies in heaven. Christ's offering for our guilt was not simply "acceptable" in God's sight, as though it were one good option in the midst of multiple choices for our atonement. It was the will of the Lord to crush him. Think of it! The eternal Son of God, the second person of the Trinity, was not merely open to the plan from eternity past for his crushing, grieving, and death on the cross. The Son agreed to the Father's plan of redemption and endured the cross for the joy set before him.

Was Jesus missing something in and of himself? Why does the text say he was made perfect through suffering? The perfection this passage speaks of is not a moral perfection. The Bible clearly teaches that Jesus is sinless. Hebrews 5:8–9 gives us insight into this perfection: "Although he was a son, he learned obedience through what he suffered. And being made perfect, he became the source of eternal salvation to all who obey him." Obedience unto death on a cross for the sins of many is the obedience learned by the Son. At the cross his obedience was completely tested, and on the third day Jesus finished his course and was raised from the dead to incorruptible glory.

It was fitting for the Son to achieve his proven, perfect obedience to the Father through the cross. The cross and its results are utterly fitting because that's why Jesus came. The Father sent the Son into the world to be crucified and resurrected so that he could bring "many sons to glory." When the first Adam selfishly sinned, he led all his sons to death. By the grace of God, when the sinless last Adam gave his own life, he tasted death for everyone, was resurrected to new creation life forever, and gets to see his offspring. Jesus deserves the reward of his suffering—a great multitude that no one could number, from every nation, from all tribes and peoples and languages (Rev. 7:9).

It is fitting because it was the Lord's will. If the Lord has willed something, then it must be good in the deepest, truest sense of the word. Do you believe that? In your heart of hearts do you agree that whatever the Lord wills is right and good, and unquestionably, ultimately *good* because he is good?

Friend, it takes faith to believe this and to walk in this every day.

The Big *Why* Question of Motherhood

Why am I doing this? This is the question—spoken or unspoken—that we ask ourselves as we persevere through the labor of expecting a child and daily mothering our children. What is our driving hope when we struggle—annual Mother's Day brunches? Seeing our kids off to good universities? A house full of future grandchildren?

Day and night, why do we give ourselves away?

Because of the gospel. This stunning portrait of the Suffering Servant shapes a Christ-centered perspective for our motherhood. Every theme of pain and suffering in this world gives way to a vision of our glorious Christ.

Friend, every one of us suffers loss in various ways and is tempted to think we are the less for it. We blame God for our pain and throw away our confident faith instead of persevering by grace through faith. Where we have failed in our trials and groaned in our self-sacrifice for our kids, Jesus endured the cross for the joy set before him. In our calling as moms we are willing to suffer these various losses with the hope of glory because this Jesus—the Suffering Servant—is the founder of the salvation we enjoy.

Our willingness to sacrificially lay down our wants and needs for the sake of our children's good (when the world would insist that we crawl off the altar and refuse to lay our lives down) is our testimony of confidence in our powerful God to lead us through death to self and death itself into glory.

10

The Birth Pains of Death

Men of Israel, hear these words: Jesus of Nazareth, a man attested to you by God with mighty works and wonders and signs that God did through him in your midst, as you yourselves know—this Jesus, delivered up according to the definite plan and foreknowledge of God, you crucified and killed by the hands of lawless men. God raised him up, loosing the pangs of death, because it was not possible for him to be held by it.

Acts 2:22–24

It's the announcement that a mother trembling in birth pain can utter and cause everyone else to tremble with anticipation. "The baby is coming!"

At this point in the labor process, the initial minutes and hours of contractions (however short or long they lasted) have given way to what is called the transition phase. Under typical circumstances this phase is rather intense for everyone involved. The medical professionals who are present may busy themselves with getting ready. Supporters find themselves cheering, "Push!" I once heard a midwife counsel an expectant father during this time, "Don't be worried about what [the mother] says—it's the labor talking." One push away from the birth of one of my own kids I announced that I was tired of laboring and please excuse me because I'm leaving now.

When Jesus's Hour Had Come

As you read the Bible, and all of the mentions of "birth pain" start to jump out at you—the rock at Meribah, God's enemies, Israel, the cross, creation, Paul and church planting, death itself —you begin to wonder who or what is *not* described by the metaphor of birth pain!

When the hour had come for Jesus to go to the cross, he knew it. We know that Jesus was not ignorant of the time because, as Peter puts it, Jesus was delivered up according to the definite plan and foreknowledge of God. He knew it because his Father planned it from eternity past, and he agreed to it. The hour that was coming for Jesus was the hour of God's judgment for our sin. Jesus had said a week earlier, "Now is my soul troubled. And what shall I say? 'Father, save me from this hour'? But for this purpose I have come to this hour" (John 12:27).

The night he allowed himself to be led away by a mob to a series of unjust trials and his imminent crucifixion, the Man who designed birth used the language of birth to describe the nature of resurrection joy: "When a woman is giving birth, she has sorrow because her hour has come, but when she has delivered the baby, she no longer remembers the anguish, for joy that a human being has been born into the world" (John 16:21).

A shepherd-boy-turned-king once wrote about a time when Yahweh delivered him. Dated approximately two hundred years before Jesus, the Greek translation of Psalm 18:4 says, "The birth pains of death encompassed me." Wait, did he say that death had . . . *birth* pain? What a curious thought. David restates what he means in other phrases such as "torrents of destruction" (v. 4) and "snares of death" (v. 5). See, it isn't actually the case that death experienced birth pain, but that birth pain here would lead to David's death, just like the "torrents" and "snares" would lead to his destruction. Yahweh delivered David from death in that moment, and David lived to write Psalm 18.

Then hundreds of years later, a fisherman-turned-apostle stood in the temple complex and used that phrase, arguing that Yahweh resurrected the Messiah by loosing the birth pains of death. Jesus had been crucified for our sin; it was Christ and no other who bore our judgment and physically died in our place. Peter was a firsthand witness to the fact that Jesus physically died. When Jesus submitted himself to the wrath of God against our sin on the cross, he was forsaken by God and his heart stopped beating and brain activity ceased. Jesus really died. And Peter was also a firsthand witness to the fact that Jesus physically rose from the dead. The birth pains of death produced death on the cross, but it was not possible for the Righteous One to be held by death. Three days later God loosed the birth pains of death and raised Jesus up. Jesus really rose from the dead!

Bursting the Birth Pains of Death

No one took Jesus's life from him—he laid it down. One night at bedtime my kindergarten-aged son asked, "Did Jesus know the cross was going to work or did he make a guess?" Yes,

Jesus knew—he always knew because it was always God's plan. Friend, believe it!

There was never any possibility that Jesus would remain entombed in that garden grave. Jesus went to the cross fully on purpose with the resurrection in mind not only with his Father's approval and blessing, but because of his charge: "No one takes it from me, but I lay it down of my own accord. I have authority to lay it down, and I have authority to take it up again. This charge I have received from my Father" (John 10:18).

When Peter argued in his sermon at Pentecost that Christ had burst through the birth pain of death into resurrection life, the implication was clear: Jesus brought our human flesh out of the grave and into immortal life, making him the first man ("firstborn") in the new creation. Because the cords of death could not hold our Savior, that means those who are in him will also be raised from the dead.

Since Jesus has risen from the dead, we can trust him as we walk through the valleys of where the shadows of death play on the wall. Through death Jesus destroyed the Devil, the one who has the power of death. The risen Christ says, "Fear not, I am the first and the last, and the living one. I died, and behold I am alive forevermore, and I have the keys of Death and Hades" (Rev. 1:17–18).

That's why we don't grieve like we're hopeless, even if a woman or child is overcome by death in the process of childbirth. We grieve deeply. But we do not grieve as those who do not have hope, for the day is coming when the One who overcame the pangs of death will bring to life again those who have fallen asleep. He will not leave us or our dear ones in the grave (1 Thess. 4:13–14).

Jesus is risen from the dead, and new creation life is springing up out of the ashes in every dark corner of the globe. The seemingly insurmountable joy of waiting for a baby to be born or come home will be swiftly surpassed when we see the culmination of various labors (Jesus building his church, God redeeming creation, the Spirit's fruit borne through us) in the new creation. All our groanings will end when we finally see what we've been hoping for, as the consummation of God's promised restoration bursts forth in full. Until that day we tremble in hopeful anticipation.

11

Jesus's Death Begets Spiritual Offspring

"Sing, O barren one, who did not bear;
    break forth into singing and cry aloud,
    you who have not been in labor!
For the children of the desolate one will be more
    than the children of her who is married," says the LORD.

Isaiah 54:1

Know then that it is those of faith who are the sons of Abraham.

Galatians 3:7

Can't remember where you put your tea cup from this morning? Don't know what you wanted to check when you clicked on the calendar app? Not sure who asked you to do someth . . . or if you've read this chapter yet? Friend, if you're experiencing the phenomenon known as "mommy brain," then you'll appreciate this prayer from Jonathan Edwards. He prayed simply, "Lord, stamp eternity on my eyeballs." Mommy brain or no, we all need reminders to think about our lives in light of forever.

Thinking deeply about the foreknowledge and predestination of God is one of those eternity-focusing lenses. Whether you're used to looking at things from this vantage point already or not doesn't matter because the Word of God is a one-size-fits-all perspective corrector.

Speaking of foreknowledge and plans, I realize that the possibility exists that perhaps you didn't plan this baby or the timing or the circumstances that surround the child. Maybe everything is going exactly as you planned, perhaps you're happy to adjust the vision you had for your life and family, or maybe you're really, really struggling. Friend, you're in good company; we all need help to keep our hope where it belongs.

Parenthood Planned Before Time

While we see things from our time-bound, spatially limited viewpoint at any given moment, God can see all of history (which he has planned) laid bare before him always. This is why I love thinking about the foreknowledge and predestination of God as it relates to the subject at hand: pregnancy, birth, and motherhood.

Do you find yourself winded by the rigors of pregnancy and motherhood? Friend, the passage we're meditating on today will take your breath away. Isaiah 54 is a picture of God's never-changing intention to fill the earth with his glory through his Son. The power by which he always intended to accomplish this is his gospel.

We've already noted that biological procreation was necessary for the fulfilling of the creation mandate in Genesis 1:28. As we walk through the Bible, we must know that it all points to Jesus. Isaiah shows us how the charge to "fill the earth" is fulfilled in "the Servant"—that is, in Jesus. Isaiah prophesied the death of the Servant, which would mark a cataclysmic shift in salvation history and be the means by which he fills the earth with God's glory.

The Servant atones for the sins of his people, bearing their griefs and sorrows. He is wounded and crushed not for his own sin, but in order to bring healing to sinners. His sin-bearing would make the guilty righteous and the unclean clean. But his sufferings would not be the end for him. Whereas the marred, rejected, and oppressed One was taken away by judgment, his victory is seen by all, as he "shall see his offspring," is "high and lifted up, and shall be exalted," and receives "the spoil with the strong" (Isa. 52:13; 53:10–12). The culmination of suffering is death, but the Servant is vindicated in every way. Jesus's sufferings are actually *the means by which* he bears offspring. The cross is the place where his victory is shared with the multitude from every nation.

Now back to Isaiah 54:1. The "barren one" here is Sarah, the wife of Abraham, and this prophecy refers to the promise God made to Abraham. Specifically, the promise included making Abraham into a great nation and a blessing to all the families of the earth. Sarah was barren, but she believed that God was faithful to keep the promise he made to Abraham. By faith she received power to conceive well past the time her "biological clock" said time was up (Heb. 11:11).

So, with the Abrahamic blessing in view, the prophecy in Isaiah 54 told the people that God will fulfill his promise to Abraham. Israel would be restored from their current captivity, and something unprecedented was around the corner, namely "the children of the desolate one will be more than the children of her who is married."

Inconceivable?

Paul explains in simple terms that Jesus is *the* true seed of Abraham. In Jesus all the nations of the earth are blessed as they are included in him by faith. "Now the promises were made to Abraham and to his offspring. It does not say, 'And to offsprings,' referring to many, but referring to one, 'And to your offspring,' who is Christ" (Gal. 3:16).

"Father Abraham had many sons," as the song goes, but there is one Son whose children will out-populate the stars that twinkle in the sky. By grace through faith are we among those children. God saved Abraham by counting his faith as righteousness so that everyone who would be numbered among Abraham's offspring would be sons by faith alone (see Rom. 4:1–12 and Gal. 3:7–9).

We're "blood-related" sons of Abraham through the blood of Jesus, shed for us on the cross. Jesus is the fulfillment of this prophecy of unparalleled fruitfulness. Through his death and resurrection he is the first one to live out Isaiah 54:1, and now by his Spirit he is multiplying "heirs according to promise" (Gal. 3:29). Where everyone else failed in carrying out the creation mandate, Isaiah 54 teaches us that God is keeping his promises through spiritual Israel's end-time King.

Jesus is the only one who could do this. We know that because of Adam's sin, Adam became spiritually impotent to carry out the spiritual procreation of spreading the glory of God throughout the world. Because of his sin, Adam needed a Redeemer to deliver him from his sin and all of his children from their sin. Human history did not and will not end in miserable failure, because the last Adam foreknew and created the first Adam and would profusely succeed where the first had failed. Now how's that for an afternoon eternal-perspective-shaping thought?

Isn't it a delightful wonder that the Lord uses childbirth terminology to teach us what it means to be part of his creation in Christ? "Enlarge the place of your tent. . . . For you will spread abroad to the right and to the left" (Isa. 54:2–3) directs our gaze to Jesus, who gave us this charge before he ascended back into heaven: "Go therefore and make disciples of all nations" (Matt. 28:19).

Everything got flip-turned upside down at Easter. The same Spirit of God who raised Jesus from death into new creation life is currently causing the offspring of the barren one's Son—men, women, and children from every tribe—to be born again to a living hope.

12

Birth Pain after Childbirth to Raise Spiritual Disciples

My little children, for whom I am again in the anguish of childbirth until Christ is formed in you!

Galatians 4:19

Jesus gets the credit for giving Nayana the idea. Our kids were in the same preschool class that year, but we hadn't met each other until the teacher connected us. Prompted by the Lord, Nayana had raised this topic with the teacher: spiritual conversations with children. And prompted by the Lord, the teacher then introduced me and Nayana to each another. We soon met for coffee at a playground while my toddler toddled. I was refreshed to hear Nayana's testimony, and my heart leaped as she described how she was teaching her daughters about Jesus. "If I have spent so much time waiting to have a friend to talk about these things," she reasoned, "then how many more mothers are in the same position?" I agreed.

Now, a few years on, a small group of moms have been meeting in my living room to read the Bible and pray for each other, our kids, and the community. The Lord has so knit our hearts together that when we pray for each others' kids, it is as though we're in anguished prayer over our own children. Last week one mother shared an update on her college-aged son and another mom was beaming when she exclaimed, "Oh, I just *love* him!" Later, another mom piped in as still another mom asked for prayer for her college-aged son: "I still haven't met him yet, but I love him, too!" My soul is encouraged each week I meet with this gathering of moms who rejoice with moms who rejoice and weep with moms who weep.

It's easier to press on in parenting when you have like-minded mothers who are *with* you. If our labor in raising our kids was just a matter of diaper-changing and food-cooking, we could simply hire a staff for domestic work and the burden would be lifted. We sometimes talk that way, but is extra hands to help really all we need? There is so much more to our mothering work than meets the eye. Our hope is not merely that our children would be fed, clothed, and educated, but our desire is that they would be nourished by God's Word, clothed in the righteousness of Christ, and taught to fear the Lord. Even after we give birth, we are still in labor.

The Ongoing Writhing of Making Disciples

Paul spoke of his ministry to the Galatians as being in birth pain to see Christ formed in them. He sacrificed and suffered to see the Galatians grow into spiritual maturity. Similarly, our aim is that our children would be children of God, and we should press on daily to see Christ formed in our children. Laboring for our children didn't end when they were born.

The birth language Paul uses here gives us the picture of spiritual agony. Painful contractions are ongoing until birth is accomplished. He addresses them as "my little children," not my unborn children who have yet to be born again, but my little children. These disciples of Jesus were already born again, but Paul feels like he is *again* in anguish over their birth as he combats dangerous false teaching. For him to use such dramatic terms is not exaggerating the case at hand because eternal life and death truly are at stake.

But even if Paul labors for them unto his own death, can Paul save these people finally? No, it is Jesus's death that produces spiritual offspring. Paul knows this well, for it is the gospel he clearly preaches. His labor, then, is his sacrificial life of suffering to see the Galatians grow into maturity. So can we, as mothers, save our children by our labors? What if we give our own bodies, as many mothers have throughout the years, in order that our child may live? Will this ultimate sacrifice be enough?

Spiritual Formation Is a Community Project

You might be familiar with the promise of God recorded in Romans 8:28: "And we know that for those who love God all things work together for good, for those who are called according to his purpose."

What an incredible thought! Grab ahold of this truth and cling to it for dear life—it will hold your heart steady when you wonder if "all things" includes the things you are currently facing or will someday face. And in your promise-clinging, do not forget the purpose—God's purpose for which he is working. It's right there in the next verse: "For those whom he foreknew he also predestined to be conformed to the image of his Son, in order that he might be the firstborn among many brothers" (Rom. 8:29).

If we are honest with ourselves, we admit that we want our own custom-made, hand-picked sanctification plan (for us and for our kids). We're willing to identify one or two areas of our lives that have yet to be conformed to Christ. We're willing to settle for some faith-testing trials (but not *too* fiery), lots of edifying relationships (but not *too* intense), and maybe even one humbling thorn in the flesh (but not *too* deep or sharp). But God is after the complete transformation of his children, and praise the Lord that he will not stop until we are conformed to the image of his Son.

God is after godly offspring because Jesus is destined to be the firstborn among many brothers who love like he loves, think like he thinks, and serve like he serves. This is God's goal for you, dear Christian sister, and for all whom he has predestined. The church is one great, big family of brothers and sisters. We are alive together with Christ even as we die to ourselves every day, and will one day be physically raised from death like Jesus was raised. Our heavenly Father has lovingly appointed for us the way he brings about this character-conforming in each of our lives. Our place is not to criticize him, but to gratefully submit to him.

And we do this together! "Mature manhood" is a synonym Paul uses for the end goal of the Christian life (Eph. 4:13). This is no individual man growing up into manhood, but the new humanity ("we all") that will one day attain to the stature of the fullness of Christ. That's what Paul wants for the church—Christ formed in us. By grace we cling to the gospel every day, and by grace we hold out this same gospel to our kids. It's the rhythm of the Christian life—every day we beat that drum and live according to it by faith. Discipleship is a painful labor—both for us and the women who disciple us and make disciples alongside us—but we know the saying is trustworthy and deserving of full acceptance, that Christ Jesus came into the world to save sinners, of whom I am the foremost (1 Tim. 1:15).

13

Putting Pain in Its Place

So we do not lose heart. Though our outer self is wasting away, our inner self is being renewed day by day. For this light momentary affliction is preparing for us an eternal weight of glory beyond all comparison, as we look not to the things that are seen but to the things that are unseen. For the things that are seen are transient, but the things that are unseen are eternal.

2 Corinthians 4:16–18

It is remarkably easy to wallow in misery. Nobody likes misery in and of itself, but it's a different story if someone notices your miserable circumstances, isn't it? Sometimes all it takes is a word of sympathy. Someone says, "That must be really hard for you," and we're shaking our heads like the melancholy donkey in the classic children's books by A. A. Milne. *Thanks for noticin' me. Could be worse. Not sure how, but it could be.*

A well-intentioned, outward-focused comment from a friend is distorted by our self-centered hearts as affirmation that we are, indeed, being slighted by the universe.

I catch myself doing this, and I hate it. What someone means as a blessing or a mere observation—"You have your hands full with your kids"—gets twisted by my heart into fodder for a mommy martyr complex. *Mmhmm, preach, sister. I'm breaking my back over here, and it's high time somebody noticed.* Oh friend, what is it about our nurturing work that tests our hearts in this way? It's service we (mostly) love to do for the benefit of the people we (imperfectly) love. So why is it so hard to mother others with steadfast hearts full of love?

Searching for Real Hope

If you feel this tension, praise the Lord! It's a grace to realize that you need grace for your motherhood and wake up every day saying, "Lord, I can't do this without you." It's hard to nurture our children and not lose heart because life in a fallen world is hard. Our lives are replete with hardships of various kinds. Fake hope is like using toothpaste to spackle a hole in the wall. It's a poor filler for that cavity, and all you get in the end is a colony of ants with minty breath. This is a goofy illustration, but it's a fraction of how goofy we look when we patch up our need for enduring hope with solutions that don't last.

This has been discussed briefly already, but it bears repeating here: our pain is not meritorious. Using pain as a pedestal to boost our ego is one of those fake hope solutions that doesn't last. When pain builds our pride, then the diagnosis is that we have a heart problem, and the gospel is the cure. The Son of God bore the wrath of his Father and bled his heart out on the cross so that we might be liberated from bondage to sin.

When we stop building our pedestals of maternal glory (and stop looking sideways at other moms), we can direct our focus somewhere else entirely. Wavering hearts find lasting hope only when they look to Christ.

In our passage above Paul presents a dichotomy of focus—the seen and the unseen. Now, if there's anyone in the world whose daily life is filled with all things "seen," then it is mothers. (Remember: this isn't fodder for our mommy martyr complex!) You're surprised by an empty pantry and turn into a prosecuting attorney when the next person enters the kitchen. You see Mount Laundry about to erupt with cotton blends, and the thought occurs that your family is trying to bury you. You see morning light peeking under the curtains, and you've already had enough. These may be exaggerations of our responses to what is seen (or they may not be). How can we keep our focus on Christ while our outer selves are wasting away at breakneck speed?

On the Other Side of the Groaning

Paul wants us to see the connection between what we see in front of us and what we are really looking for—the (yet) unseen hope of glory. We'll talk more about this passage in the next chapter, but it is good to start thinking about it now: "For we know that the whole creation has been groaning together in the pains of childbirth until now. And not only the creation, but we ourselves, who have the firstfruits of the Spirit, groan inwardly as we wait eagerly for adoption as sons, the redemption of our bodies" (Rom. 8:22–23).

Friend, picture it. Paul is saying that a mother in the throes of labor helps us understand that our suffering in this life is far outweighed by the joy we will experience in the resurrection. Everything in the realm of the "seen"—the sweat, tears, uncertainty, anticipation, pain, groaning—gives way to the yet "unseen"—the profound relief and joy you feel when everyone hears the sound of a wailing baby. Whether or not she is aware of it, a mom in labor is a picture of eschatological hope. She perseveres through contraction after contraction with endurance because of what happens after labor is over: delivery. One of my friends said, "I'm not scheduling my Cesarean section because it sounds like a fun way to spend a Friday. I just want to hold my sweet baby."

God doesn't ordain our pain so we can pat ourselves on the back. Fertility struggles, marital stress, pregnancy and labor, adoption complications, the struggle of being a sinner who is raising sinners in a fallen world—even when our eyes are blurry with tears, we see with eyes of faith that God has purposed our suffering to produce an incomparably glorious outcome. When we undergo light and momentary affliction in our mothering, then we see it for what it is—a reminder to look to the unseen. Birth is not about us, but about God.

Are you *fighting* to not lose heart today? Be encouraged! It's so easy to give in and be obsessed with the outer self that is wasting away. We're so content to dig, research, interview, and pursue fixes to the transient decay everywhere around us. We take care of the transient, but we don't throw our hearts into it. Let's be obsessed with what we're going to be obsessed with thirty zillion years from now: the glory of Jesus. That's bona fide hope. And we know it's real because our inner self is being renewed day by day.

14

All Creation in the Throes of Labor

For nation will rise against nation, and kingdom against kingdom, and there will be famines and earthquakes in various places. All these are but the beginning of the birth pains.

Matthew 24:7–8

For we know that the whole creation has been groaning together in the pains of childbirth until now. And not only the creation, but we ourselves, who have the first-fruits of the Spirit, groan inwardly as we wait eagerly for adoption as sons, the redemption of our bodies. For in this hope we were saved. Now hope that is seen is not hope. For who hopes for what he sees? But if we hope for what we do not see, we wait for it with patience.

Romans 8:22–25

Perhaps you've seen videos on the Internet of men voluntarily undergoing simulations of artificial birth pain. In the beginning of one such video two men are seen laughing, and at the end of the experiment they're doubled over, weeping. If men in birth pain is a peculiar-sounding idea, how about the cosmos?

As we saw in the previous chapter, our suffering in this present age produces for us a future glory. But there is more to see in the metaphor of childbirth. As curious as it seems to think of it, in a very real sense all creation is currently being throttled by unrelenting birth pain. All creation. From the starry host in the night sky to the earth's metallic core. Nations, kingdoms, famines, earthquakes. And not only is the old creation groaning, but so are we who have the first gift of the *new* creation—the Holy Spirit. Together with creation we're groaning in the pains of a particular kind of childbirth.

It's good from time to time to step back and remember that all of these biblical references to childbirth point us to God. It is not as though God has merely taken notice of the human activity of childbearing and spontaneously reacted to it like a good teacher. He hasn't merely turned human birth into an object lesson to creatively speak truth into our lives about himself. Rather, God is the Creator who has wisely designed all things, and we are made in his image. Our birth pain is like God's, not the other way around (recall chap. 7).

Nothing is incidental in God's creation—he created all things to bring him glory. Fish covered in leopard-print gliding along on the ocean floor. Plants that grow on other plants that grow on other plants. Clouds that materialize on the horizon and move along with the wind. Image bearers of the triune God crawling, toddling, walking, rolling, flying, being carried around the planet—multiplying, building, designing, problem-solving, dreaming, loving. We see God's invisible attributes in the things he has made, and the only correct response is to worship him. Jesus has written us into his story, and he designed birth to glorify himself.

The Presence of the Spirit Induces Our Groaning

The Bible contains many instances of the birth metaphor to teach us about God. In our passages above we learn that all creation is experiencing the agony of birth pain as it waits for its ultimate renewal at the end of the age. Birth pain is a picture of how a Christian awaits final glory.

The ground really is cursed, but it really will be redeemed and made new. History really is going somewhere, and things are not yet the way they will forever be. The pain of life in this fallen world is no false labor. The hardest part, perhaps, is to realize that the transition phase could last many more millennia until the Lord's return. (Or he could return tomorrow, and the birth pains transform into exultant rejoicing when the new creation comes in full.) People from every tribe and tongue who have the Holy Spirit are new creation, and his presence in the world facilitates our eschatological groaning.

The Spirit is the "first gift" or "firstfruits" because he is given to be the down payment of our inheritance from our Father (Eph. 1:14). If you are a believer in Jesus, it is the Spirit who has awoken you from death and is leading you as you groan until the revealing of all the children of God in glory. The Spirit was given to you to help you discern good and evil, to keep your mind swirling with thoughts about eternity, to share his certainty with you of Christ's imminent return, and to lead you in the freedom from sin that Jesus purchased for you. He teaches you to pray, "Abba! Father!," and holds your heart steady when the birth pains of creation and your own groaning make you want to give up. The Spirit is with you in your pain, comforting you with Christ's peace that surpasses understanding. *Jesus is with you. He is coming soon. Then we will always be with the Lord!* Don't neglect the Spirit-facilitated urge to groan for Christ's return.

And dear one who is still considering the claims of Christ, thank God for the compassion he is showing you as his Spirit patiently does his work. It is the Spirit who is convicting you of your sin before a holy God. The Spirit is attesting to Christ's righteousness so you can see him for who he truly is. He presses on your heart and mind the urgency of your need for salvation from your sin in the face of coming judgment. Hear the invitation from the Spirit and from the church, who is called "the bride of Christ": "The Spirit and the Bride say, 'Come,' And let the one who hears say, 'Come.' And let the one who is thirsty come; let the one who desires take the water of life without price" (Rev. 22:17). You're so thirsty, friend, and you know all of the wells of this world are cracked and leaking and polluted. Will you come and drink from the Lord, who is a fountain of living water? Would you even now exchange your trust in the things that you see for a hope that will not disappoint?

Maybe you know what it feels like to birth a baby out of your physical body; maybe you don't. Maybe this is something you long for, or not. The phenomenon of birth pain points all of us—all of us—to deeply consider the picture God has given us. It's a picture of what it looks like to wait in pain for a redemption that you can't see yet. He loves us, and he wants us to know beyond a shadow of a doubt that hope *will* give way to sight. God's labor over creation and his children will not stall out—he will finish what he started. My hope is that we all would be among those who love the day of Christ's coming and wait for him with patient, faith-full hearts even while we groan in this world.

15

Conceived in Sin and Saved by Grace

For I know my transgressions,
    and my sin is ever before me.
Against you, you only, have I sinned
    and done what is evil in your sight,
so that you may be justified in your words
    and blameless in your judgment.
Behold, I was brought forth in iniquity,
    and in sin did my mother conceive me.

Psalm 51:3–5

Do you know what David did? The grievous sins he committed are recorded in unbreakable Scripture for all to read (see 2 Samuel 11). Coveting, lust, adultery, stealing, lying, murder by proxy. In the passage above David isn't just repenting of these sins; he's acknowledging the root of his sinfulness and asking for mercy.

"In sin did my mother conceive me." No, he's not blaming his mom and dad; he's accepting personal blame for his sins. David is confessing that because he is part of the human race, he has been a sinner from his conception. David is going way back to his first parents—Adam and Eve. Adam, the representative head of humanity, failed and sinned against God. And that explains why he, David, was born that way—hopelessly lost and dead in his sin. David's problem is our problem, too. It's my problem, your problem, and all of our kids' problem. Our sin is ever before us.

I realize that at this point you might not want to read any more of this chapter. It just doesn't seem fair. For one man to do something and bring down all of his future children with him into death doesn't sound fair. I hope you'll keep reading and see something else that wasn't "fair." Another Man did something and brought all of his future children up with him from death.

Can We Talk about the Garden Again?

Adam's sin concerning the tree in the garden powerfully catapulted all his seed into dark death. Sin came into God's good creation unlawfully and had no right to enter, and it didn't happen by accident. Thanks to the willful disobedience of our representative, the entire human race is guilty of sin against God. The seeds of sin are sown in our hearts, inherited from our parents, and passed down to our children.

It is globally unpopular to believe we are born with this original sin nature, but the Bible plainly teaches it. "They have all fallen away; together they have become corrupt; there is none who does good, not even one" (Ps. 53:3). What else can explain the universality and extent of our depravity? "Who can say, 'I have made my heart pure; I am clean from my sin'?" (Prov. 20:9). "Surely there is not a righteous man on earth who does good and never sins" (Eccles. 7:20). Our ability to "learn sin" through nurture and habit cannot account for the crushing power that sin has over all humanity. Our willpower isn't weak; it ravenously craves what is not good. "What is man, that he can be pure? Or he who is born of a woman, that he can be righteous?" (Job 15:14). We are all "by nature children of wrath, like the rest of mankind" (Eph. 2:3).

We're all sinners from our conception who are born into a process of dying. We come into this world spiritually stillborn. Every part of us is hell-bent on pursuing what God hates. Eyes absorbing things we shouldn't see. Feet taking us places we shouldn't go. Fingers texting things we shouldn't write. Mouths and tongues uttering what we should not say and setting our lives on fire. Our desperately sick hearts pumping out all manner of unrighteousness.

And then when our guilty conscience takes us through the wringer every day, we ignore it, pacify it with some form of religiosity, and justify ourselves. We aren't simply products of our environment who spontaneously or habitually commit sins. We *are* sinners. Human sinfulness extends to our whole selves. God is blameless when he judges. Against God, God only, every one of us has sinned.

Every one us except for *One*.

His Mercy Is More

You likely know what I am about to say now, but doesn't it bear repeating again and again? This gospel is the soundtrack of our lives—playing on repeat, louder and louder. We need to hear it every day, and so do our kids. Why do we need the gospel? Because there is no viable alternative. There is one God, and there is *one* mediator between God and men, the man Christ Jesus (1 Tim. 2:5).

Jesus is the last Adam, whose obedience at the cross is far more powerful than our sin and has a far greater effect: "For if, because of one man's trespass, death reigned through that one man, much more will those who receive the abundance of grace and the free gift of righteousness reign in life through the one man Jesus Christ" (Rom. 5:17).

Much more! Much more! Yes, our sin wreaks havoc in our lives and causes death, but the grace and righteousness of Jesus gives us so *much more* than what our sin destroyed. The obedience of Jesus at the cross much more powerfully catapulted all his seed into eternal life. "For as by the one man's disobedience the many were made sinners, so by the one man's obedience the many will be made righteous" (Rom. 5:19). In Christ we are slaves to righteousness, at war with our sin, renewing our minds, approving of the law of God, worshiping our Creator in spirit and truth, walking in good deeds, discerning God's will, receiving God's wisdom, submitting to Christ's authority, longing to love God with all our heart, and reveling in *true* freedom to be who we were made to be.

Bask in This Hope!

Dear reader, are your thoughts cruelly ruled by your fears? Is your heart anxiously preoccupied with avoiding shame? Does your guilty conscience throw your sins in your face? Are you whitewashing your soul with religion in hopes that the gnawing death you feel inside will disappear? Have you received grace from God only to thank him that you are not like "other" moms? Do you see these tendencies in the lives of your children?

When our first parents sinned in the garden, they were taken captive by shame and fear, knew they were guilty, and tried to hide from the only One who could save them. But God! Even while they were still sinners, God loved them, pursued them, and brought them back into a relationship with him. His gospel gives us—and our kids—hope!

God is reversing spiritual death as he redeems men, women, and children from every tribe on the planet out of this old age and into his new creation. Jesus is being fruitful and multiplying his offspring, filling and blessing the world. These redeemed image bearers therefore go and carry the message of the gospel with them as they witness to a lost world. Every day they remember the cross and the price God paid for their redemption. They remember that after Jesus was crucifed and laid in the tomb, Jesus rose from the dead three days later. The tomb is empty! This means death's tyranny is over and the day is coming when physical death will be reversed, too.

How will this reversal come about? Our sinful condition is so helplessly bad that even a second chance with a fresh start won't do the trick. We need *new* birth.

16

You Must Be Born Again

Now there was a man of the Pharisees named Nicodemus, a ruler of the Jews. This man came to Jesus by night and said to him, "Rabbi, we know that you are a teacher come from God, for no one can do these signs that you do unless God is with him." Jesus answered him, "Truly, truly, I say to you, unless one is born again he cannot see the kingdom of God." Nicodemus said to him, "How can a man be born when he is old? Can he enter a second time into his mother's womb and be born?" Jesus answered, "Truly, truly, I say to you, unless one is born of water and the Spirit, he cannot enter the kingdom of God. That which is born of the flesh is flesh, and that which is born of the Spirit is spirit. Do not marvel that I said to you, 'You must be born again.' The wind blows where it wishes, and you hear its sound, but you do not know where it comes from or where it goes. So it is with everyone who is born of the Spirit."

John 3:1–8

I adore puns. (We all have our quirks, right?) One of my favor-ite occasions to be punny is when introducing myself to a group of people. In our diverse context it's typical to start with where you're from, so when it's my turn to contribute to the conversa-tion I say, "Well, I was born at an early age [cue the laughter and eye-rolling] in the United States." On some occasions I add, "But I was born again at age eighteen in Texas." Cue the raised eyebrows and questions!

To be *born again* is actually not a play on words—it is a spiritual reality. We've discussed in this book how God is the Creator of everything, including childbirth. How delightfully mind-boggling it is to meditate on the fact that God ordained everything from eternity past! From the East Australian Cur-rent to the wanderings of nomadic people groups in the Gobi Desert, all things are from him and through him and to him. In one sense childbirth is an ordinary phenomenon. After all, childbirth has happened to us all (billions of us!). How many women all over the world are laboring to give birth as you read these words? In another sense, childbirth is beyond compare. The triumph of life over pain, struggle, and even death itself touches our hearts.

In this passage Jesus is teaching us how to trace those pro-verbial dust particles that dance in the sunbeam up to the glori-ous sun itself. There's a gigantic sun of spiritual reality that we need to be aware of, and God designed childbirth to help open our eyes to see it.

The Answer We All Need to the Question We Don't Know to Ask

Although Nicodemus didn't see it coming, Jesus foresaw, planned, and orchestrated their late-night conversation about . . . birth. Imagine. You're out for an evening stroll, and you pass by your neighbor's house. Male voices echo through the courtyard as one man asks another man, "Can a man enter a second time into his mother's womb?" You might be inclined to stop and listen in on that conversation.

In God's kindness, we do get to listen in on that conversation here in the Gospel of John. Did you notice that Nicodemus didn't lead with an explicit question for Jesus? But Jesus responded to him with an answer—*the* answer—to Nicodemus's greatest problem. *You must be born again.* It's the singular, compulsory solution to the problem we all have. And if new birth is the answer, then the corresponding problem is that we are helplessly not alive. "And you were dead in the trespasses and sins" (Eph. 2:1). You cannot be more spiritually helpless than *dead*. Apart from the new birth, you're not a woman treading water in the waves looking for a life vest; you're as spiritually lifeless as a corpse in the silt on the ocean floor.

This religious teacher's problem (and our problem) is that in this story we are not the ones who can freely bring about salvation for ourselves or others; we're the helpless ones who must be born again. Jesus doesn't tell Nicodemus "you must be born again" to show him which rung to climb on the religious ladder. He's not giving Nicodemus the shock of his life to prompt him to turn over a new leaf. "You must be born again" is the offer of eternal life. We must be called out of darkness and into the light. God must labor over our soul to make us alive together with Christ.

The Wind Blows, the Seed Scatters

But how does this new birth happen? Enter the wind. The Spirit of God is like the wind: he *freely* blows where he wishes to give life and is *capable* to bring forth life. God is the one who causes his children to be born again. How does the Spirit do this? Enter the seed: "Since you have been born again, not of perishable seed but of imperishable, through the living and abiding word of God" (1 Pet. 1:23). The apostle Peter explains that you are born again not of perishable seed (i.e., human sperm and egg) but of *imperishable seed*—through the living and abiding *Word of God*. The Spirit awakens faith, and a babe in Christ is born.

Through a meeting with your friend over tea; through a conversation at a bus stop on your commute to work; through an apology to your neighbors over what your dog did to their garden; through Bible studies in prison; through discussions in the principal's office; through your walk in the park every Thursday, where you seek to speak with whomever the Lord brings; through text messages appointed by God to illuminate a smartphone and shine light into darkness; through dreams of Jesus that compel people from other religions to seek an interpretation from a Christian; through sporadic chats with the person next to you on the elliptical machine at the gym; through debates in the break room at work; through balloons printed with Bible verses floating over the Korean demilitarized zone; through songs that exalt the person and work of Christ . . . the wind blows.

God's freedom to bring about life is . . . freeing. Maybe a lot of baggage obstructs your view of Jesus or your loved ones' views of Jesus. If that's the case, you might be feeling discouraged that more of your friends aren't turning to Jesus in repentance and faith. Maybe you aren't sure that you have new life in Christ. Oh friend, the Spirit freely blows where he wishes, and this fact encourages us to pray. Instead of feeling overwhelmed by everything on the cultural baggage carousel, pray the Spirit would move those bags out of the way and shine light on the truth. Sow the seed of the gospel and pray God would awaken faith in your friends' hearts or even your own heart. You may be praying for the upcoming birth of your baby. As you labor in prayer for this birth, pray that God would deliver their souls from death and give them new birth.

Perhaps the Spirit is in labor over *your* soul today. Did you hear the answer to your own greatest problem in Jesus's response to this religious man? Friend, if you have just become aware that you are totally incapable of saving yourself, as incapable as a baby is of bringing about its own birth, then praise God for his Spirit's work in your heart!

We all prefer to cling to the illusion that we are the master of our fate and the captain of our soul.[1] "But God, being rich in mercy, because of the great love with which he loved us, even when we were dead in our trespasses, made us alive together with Christ—by grace we have been saved" (Eph. 2:4–5). We are indeed at the mercy of a powerful and loving God. What a marvelous thing to think about—that he would design childbirth in such a way that we would have such a stark, urgent, visceral, common, and unparalleled picture of our inability to save ourselves and the Spirit's freedom to give us the life we need.

---

1. The phrase "I am the master of my fate: I am the captain of my soul" is credited to poet William Ernest Henley (1849–1903), "Invictus" in *Book of Verses* (1888).

17

Boasting Only in the Cross

But far be it from me to boast except in the cross of our Lord Jesus Christ, by which the world has been crucified to me, and I to the world.

Galatians 6:14

While self-awareness is a natural side effect of maturity, *God*-awareness is a supernatural gift of grace.

I was watching my kids take swimming lessons at the pool one afternoon when a toddler drifted by seated in a floating device and wearing a life vest. He beamed, "I swimming!" Of course, everyone in earshot melted into a puddle, and we said in chorus, "Wow! Well done!" We're inspired as we watch our children grow up through their risk-taking. We smile when they try to learn skills and encourage them: "Go on, you can do it."

Childbearing is similar to "swimming" in a life vest and floatation device. (I realize swimming might sound really lovely right now to readers who are heavily pregnant!) While we imagine ourselves to be racing against other moms in the 400-meter individual medley in the Mom Olympics, in reality we're all afloat solely because of the grace of God. If we have eyes to see, then we know how we're all carrying on in our mothering work—by grace.

Birth Teaches Us How to Boast

So if we're all afloat and empowered and sustained by grace, why do we moms boast in ourselves? Why do we assure ourselves and others with deeply believed mantras like, "You've got this"? Whatever the *this* is that we have, it's been given to us. In keeping with the swimming analogy, I think we prefer to ignore the life vest and the pool floatie *so that* we can boast in ourselves. At least, that's the case for my own heart. It is easier for me to boast in myself if I ignore the fact that everything I have is a gift.

Thankfully, God has given us childbirth to serve as a flashing, neon sign to point us to him. God is our life. He deserves the thanks and praise for everything. He is the source of it all. That's why this book labors to explain the metaphorical use of birth in Scripture. In other words, when we think about Jesus, we don't start with ourselves and our childbirth and conclude, "Jesus is like me." We see ourselves in comparison to God, not the other way around. We read the metaphorical language of birth in God's Word, and it takes our breath away when we realize that we are made to be like God. With mouths agape and hearts pounding, we wonder with the psalmist, "What is man that you are mindful of him, and the son of man that you care for him?" (Ps. 8:4).

The shining glory and grace of Jesus is *the* substantive reality of the universe. Expectant mothers—biological, adoptive, and spiritual moms included—are living pictures of the glory of Jesus. Scripture teaches us how to see childbirth as a reflection of the radiance of *Jesus*—we see as in a mirror dimly. In his inscrutable wisdom God designed conception, pregnancy, and birth to be a sign to direct our hearts to worship him, and this is not egomania—it's the height of love. From the surging luteinizing hormone to the growing baby, from the daily battle against anxiety to the thrills of hope, from the stretching skin and fluid retention to the rhythmic pain and crowning of newborn life—everything is from him and through him and to him.

But the world, in typical form, has so twisted birth that when we glimpse the wonder of it all, we dislocate worship from God back to ourselves! It's a battle to stop boasting in ourselves. Every day you pull your growing body out of bed, the world launches still more initiatives to keep you boasting in yourself, your opinions, your training, your resources, your biology, your consumer choices, and even your pain tolerance. The world around us expects moms to use these things like weapons to fight their way to the top and claim the glory we work so hard to achieve.

Can you feel the gravity of the course of this world, too? It pulls my gaze away from the glory of God in the face of Jesus Christ and fixes it squarely on my own navel. Navel-gazing while boasting in ourselves is simply the wrong vocation for women made in God's image. Weak as a puffy cloud floating overhead, the feeling of satisfaction is gone before we know it, and then we're reaching for our next glory fix.

The Best and Only Boast

But! When we behold the glory of God in the face of Jesus Christ, then we are transformed. The satisfaction, fullness, approval, and purpose we seek are realized only in Christ. When we boast in the cross—where the perfect Son of God bled and died in our place—we see him and ourselves and the world around us rightly.

For those of us who have been in Christ and discipled in his church, these things I've written may sound like a broken record. But they bear repeating because we are forgetful and weak people. Do you have eyes to behold the glory of the Lord today? Let the Bible give your heart the perspective it needs to see clearly. Movies, advertisements, and newsfeeds will not remind you that life and death are in God's hands. Feed yourself with God's Word every day to be reminded that "the LORD kills and brings to life; he brings down to Sheol and raises up" (1 Sam. 2:6). Fertility, conception, pregnancy, and birth are mercies from God—we haven't earned them or achieved them. What do we have that we did not receive from God? So how can we boast in such things?

When you're strongly tempted to boast in some aspect of your motherhood, ask yourself, "What do you have that you did not receive? Why then are you boasting?" And then remember the cost Jesus paid to give you everything you need for life and godliness. The childbirth he is giving to you or the child he has appointed for you to adopt are not about you or your glory. The best and only boast is the cross of Jesus. The cross is no shadowy, passing joy—like getting a compliment from someone or achieving a goal. It is through the shed blood of Jesus that we have eternal redemption and irrevocable forgiveness of sins. "Not to us, O LORD, not to us, but to your name give glory" (Ps. 115:1). Because of the cross we receive the lavish riches of God's grace upon grace that he loves to pour out on his daughters.

18

A Tomb Became a Womb
for the New Creation

But on the first day of the week, at early dawn, they went
to the tomb, taking the spices they had prepared. And they
found the stone rolled away from the tomb, but when they
went in they did not find the body of the Lord Jesus. While
they were perplexed about this, behold, two men stood by
them in dazzling apparel. And as they were frightened and
bowed their faces to the ground, the men said to them,
"Why do you seek the living among the dead? He is not
here, but has risen."

Luke 24:1–6

I woke this morning to eyebrow-raising headlines from all over
the world. It seems as though this day and age is full of sur-
prises. There are predictable constants, though, like the fact
that the mortality rate for all people groups everywhere is con-
sistently at 100 percent. We live and we die.

When death entered God's perfect creation through our sin, it was an unwelcome aberration to the way things were. And death is the last enemy that will be destroyed (1 Cor. 15:26).

Thinking about death's statistics puts a throbbing ache in my heart. Death's reign of horror extends even to unborn children and the mothers who carry them. While I have not personally lost a child, I know many mothers who have and a few mothers who passed away. For all of our advances in antenatal technology and postnatal care, too many women and children in the world today do not survive pregnancy and birth.

What heart can bear the sorrow of an empty crib or an empty rocking chair? The comfort we need can be found by looking into the empty tomb.

He Is Alive!

Jesus endured appalling treatment at the hands of wicked people for the cosmic rebellion that he did not commit. He was innocent through and through, but it was the will of the Lord to crush him for our sin. I remember being astonished the first time I realized that Jesus intentionally, willingly *went* to the cross. When my Bible study leaders explained to me that Christ suffered for me not under compulsion, but for my sake and in my place, I was undone. And then by God's Spirit I was born again.

On the third day Jesus rose again from the dead. The "they" in our passage above refers to several of the women who were friends of Jesus. They wanted to properly prepare his body for burial, so they went to the garden tomb with burial spices. They fully intended to apply the spices to Jesus's body because they expected to find his dead body behind the stone. That's the way things went in the old age, after all. You live and you die . . . show's over. *But not anymore.* Jesus had always intended to die on the cross for the forgiveness of our sins, and he had always intended to be raised again for our justification.

Dear friend, when Jesus became sin for us, he bore the curse for us. Behold, the Lamb of God who takes away the sin of the world! Death could not hold Jesus, and on the third day he walked out of the tomb as the first Man in the new creation. God took what was meant to be a receptacle of death and decay and turned it into the place where the new creation began to invade the old.

Jesus is alive—spiritually and bodily raised from death into eternal life by the Spirit. And the same Spirit will do the same for us. Even now he has begun his resurrection work in everyone who is in Christ. When you become a Christian, you are placed in Christ, and so in this present age you are raised spiritually. This resurrection by the Spirit is a down payment and guarantee that he will finish the good work he started—raising you bodily when Christ returns. Jesus has gone before us: "But in fact Christ has been raised from the dead, the firstfruits of those who have fallen asleep. For as by a man came death, by a man has come also the resurrection of the dead. For as in Adam all die, so also in Christ shall all be made alive" (1 Cor. 15:20–22).

Just like God's birth pain is not like ours (but our birth pain is like his), Jesus's resurrection is not like ours (but ours will be like his).

Eyes Wide Open

As mothers we have aspirations for our kids. In light of the resurrection of Jesus Christ from the grave, we can have hopes that echo in eternity. Expectant moms, as fixated as we can be on the new life growing inside us or in our hearts for our adoptive kids, the life we are to be obsessed with is resurrection life in Christ. Every morning we need to remember anew that the stone was rolled away from the tomb and the body of our crucified Lord was not there. *He is risen!* That's the hope we hold out to ourselves, and it's the hope we hold out to our kids. We've already discussed in this book that resurrection life in Christ is not something that we can earn, proselytize, or pass on genetically, but it bears repeating: salvation belongs to the Lord.

Grace would have us live with our eyes wide open to hope. When we're reeling with the nausea of living in a broken, dying world, we see with eyes of faith that resurrection is on the horizon. Press on, dear one; our anchor in the waves of sorrow is Christ himself. He suffered death for us so we would not be held by it. His nail-scarred hands unhinged the gate of the city of death. All hell could break loose on this earth but by grace through faith Jesus is ours and we are his forever.

We will see his face. We will! So now we can open our eyes each morning (plus multiple times a night in the early newborn days) and take it all in by grace. Can you imagine the first moment your eyelids open in the resurrection to behold the new creation come in full? We wake up day after pain-filled day in this broken world, but the day is coming when the last throes of this labor will be over and we will be totally, completely, thoroughly, finally newly created. Grief will turn to laughter, tears of sorrow to tears of joy.

19

Our Deliverer Delivered through Birth Pains

In those days a decree went out from Caesar Augustus that all the world should be registered. This was the first registration when Quirinius was governor of Syria. And all went to be registered, each to his own town. And Joseph also went up from Galilee, from the town of Nazareth, to Judea, to the city of David, which is called Bethlehem, because he was of the house and lineage of David, to be registered with Mary, his betrothed, who was with child. And while they were there, the time came for her to give birth. And she gave birth to her first-born son and wrapped him in swaddling cloths and laid him in a manger, because there was no place for them in the inn.

Luke 2:1–7

In eternity past God decreed that Caesar Augustus would issue his own decree. Jesus's birth story was planned from before time and prophesied for hundreds of years, but many details are hidden from recorded history.

How long was Mary's labor? Were the Bethlehem midwives on duty that night or day? Did any other moms show up to help young Mary? Did she suffer the dreaded back labor? Did the innkeeper allow Joseph to pace the floor of the inn, or did Joseph help catch the baby? We may not know the answers to such questions, but this most significant question has been clearly answered throughout the Bible: *What was God doing in a virgin's womb?*

While we wonder about the unmentioned details and rightly admire Mary's faith, we must remember the reason for the incarnation. Jesus was born a man so he could die for our sin—from the womb to a tomb. The triune Godhead conceived of a plan for the Son's cosmic rescue mission to involve his conception in a virgin's womb and his descent through the birth canal. Baby Jesus is God enfleshed in humanity with the accompanying gush of amniotic fluid and blood, attached to an umbilical cord and placenta.

Yes, friends, our Savior has a belly button. What could be more upside down to our earthly logic than his not-so-grand entrance into the world? Most world religions stick to the sterile-sounding stories. Screenwriters imagine much more fanfare when the camera pans over to the hero who has come to save the day. But God uses the weak to shame the wise—this is his way. Prophecy after prophecy points to the birth of the Messiah and how he would deliver the cosmos from bondage to sin, Satan, and death.

Born to Die

The Father's promise to send the serpent-crusher is carried out by the Holy Spirit's work to bring about the new creation. It has been rightly said that the incarnation was an invasion—the light of life blazing into the seething darkness of a chaotic

world of sin and death. The eternal Son of God was the prophesied Son of Man who came to rescue his own. "In him was
life, and the life was the light of men" (John 1:4). The eternal
Son's conception by the Spirit in the womb of a virgin was
God's "let there be light" for people walking in darkness. The
glory of the Lord shall be revealed, and all flesh shall see it together. All-glorious, adored in heaven, already at the Father's
right hand, he became flesh and dwelled among us. He who
would be delivered up for our sins was delivered through the
judgment of birth pain that we all undergo. Our slavery to
sin would soon be dealt the death blow when the Son of Man
stretched out his arms on the cross to take the penalty for
sin that we deserved. Imagine the newborn's bleating cries at
Christmas, but also imagine the chains of sin starting to rattle.

Throughout Jesus's earthly ministry the curses of the fall—
both physical and spiritual—started to fall away. Chubby infant
hands grew into calloused carpenter's hands that performed
miracles over disease, demons, fish, weather, food, a fig tree . . .
and death itself. He did these short-term miracles (even those
he raised from death would suffer death again) as signs to us
that he is *the* Promised One who would lead us out of exile,
go before us in a new exodus, and by the Spirit make all things
new—spiritually first and physically at the end of the age.

Raised Together, Enfleshed in Glory

I don't often look at the weather app on my phone unless I'm
daydreaming about the weather in Tbilisi or Rabat. This morning,
however, I wanted to see how fast the wind was blowing as another
sandstorm thrashed the palm trees in our neighborhood. During
sandstorm season the city gets pelted with microscopic pieces of
the desert for hours, leaving everything covered in dust. Outside
the window by my desk I can see newly sand-coated spider webs in

the windowsill. Those spiders aren't catching anything now! Every intricate detail of their webs is highlighted by the clinging sand against the backdrop of miniature sand dunes in the window sill corners. My window looked clear an hour ago; I had no idea the webs were there. What was hidden is now revealed.

And so it will be when believers become "incarnated" at the end of the age. Just as Jesus was vindicated in his bodily resurrection, so will everyone who is found in him be vindicated in view of the watching cosmos. Christian mom, even though you were raised together with Christ from the dead, the world does not identify you with spiritual or physical victory in this age. And of course it doesn't! Your faith in Christ the incarnate, crucified, risen, and ascended Savior is folly to them. Now they may judge you to be classless, narrow-minded, "on the wrong side of history," and weak. God's declaration of your full righteousness in Christ is invisible to the world right now. Even you, dear reader, may have your nagging doubts about God's approval of you today. But if you are *in Christ*! If you are in Christ, then your identification with him will be made manifest—physically enfleshed in glory—when the same Spirit who raised Jesus from the dead raises your body, as well.

The incarnation is the ultimate intervention, as God himself became fully entrenched in our plight but was without sin. And now by his Spirit, Jesus is newly creating us from the inside out even while we sojourn in this fallen world. What is hidden will eventually be revealed. So now, expectant mother, arise, shine; for your light has come, and the glory of the Lord has risen upon you! He who was delivered through birth pains will one day deliver the world from its birth pains when he brings his new creation in full. Our skin and flesh may be destroyed, but in our flesh we will see God—for ourselves. Our own eyes will behold him. How our hearts faint within us!

20

Saved through Childbearing

Therefore the Lord himself will give you a sign. Behold, the virgin shall conceive and bear a son, and shall call his name Immanuel.

Isaiah 7:14

But when the fullness of time had come, God sent forth his Son, born of woman, born under the law.

Galatians 4:4

Yet she will be saved through childbearing—if they continue in faith and love and holiness, with self-control.

1 Timothy 2:15

Did you just read the table of contents, and then turn directly to this page? If so, I can understand why. I probably would have done that, too, given the plethora of interpretations of this passage. Some theologians say this is the most difficult verse in the

New Testament to interpret. Depending on how you evaluate all of the grammatical nuances in this verse, you can come up with many different options for interpretation (and corresponding application).

Faithful evangelical interpreters have wrestled through each phrase of this verse and landed on suitable interpretations that differ from one another at varying points to varying degrees.[1] Who is "she"? What does it mean for her to be saved? Does the word "through" function as a means by which she is saved or a circumstance through which she is saved? The literal rendering of this verse in Greek contains an article for the word *childbearing—the* childbearing. What does "the childbearing" mean? What does "if" mean grammatically in this sentence? And finally, who are "they"?[2]

Context Is King

Selecting different answers to each of these questions might make you feel like you are reading a Choose Your Own Adventure book. In this book series you are faced with options like, "If you want the character to enter the tunnel under the pyramid, turn to page 46. If you want the character to get on a horse and ride away, turn to page 111." The shape of your adventure depends on the choices you make along the way.

Of course, this illustration breaks down because we are talking about the unchanging, eternal Word of God and not a fictional fairy tale. We are not at liberty to interpret the Bible according to our feelings. We interpret the Bible with the help of the Spirit who inspired every perfect word of it and through

---

1. The view represented in this chapter is drawn from an unpublished article, Jesse R. Scheumann, "Saved through the Childbirth of Christ (1 Tim. 2:15): Eve as the Representative Redeemed Woman in Ephesus."

2. These six questions are adapted from Stanley E. Porter, "What Does It Mean to Be 'Saved by Childbirth' (1 Timothy 2:15)?" *Journal for the Study of the New Testament*, no. 49 (1993): 88.

the practical reasoning and skills we've been given—among which "context is king." In this chapter I will briefly explain the interpretation that I think best suits the context. I ask you, gentle reader, to read charitably as I write charitably, affirming the validity of my dear brothers' and sisters' interpretations and humbly acknowledging that we all write as those who see in a mirror dimly, until we see him face to face when he returns (1 Cor. 13:12)!

From Disordered to Orderly Conduct in the Church

Our verse is found in Paul's letter to Timothy, a pastor whom Paul discipled and trained and is like a son to him. In this letter Paul writes to Timothy regarding matters of church life with accompanying instructions, encouragements, warnings, and personal updates. Chapter 2 contains instructions for corporate worship and church authority. Similar to the way he explains marriage in Ephesians 5, Paul explains his instructions on corporate worship and church authority by addressing both the men and the women and by starting at the beginning—in Genesis. His instructions to men and to women in the church are based on the creation narrative; they are consistent with what God has made and why he made it.

Paul addresses the men in 1 Timothy 2:8 with regards to their prayers and the women in verses 9 and 10 with regards to their adornment and good works. In verse 11 Paul tells Timothy to let women learn (which was radically countercultural in those days), and the way in which the women are to learn is quietly with all submissiveness. In verses 12–14 Paul reaffirms his teaching that male leadership is God's ordained pattern for the church because of creation: "For Adam was formed first, then Eve; and Adam was not deceived, but the woman was deceived and became a transgressor." Pause. Ok. So, is Paul saying that he thinks women are gullible so they're disqualified from leading in the church? No. Paul is narrating the incident in the garden of Eden—when Satan entered the serpent and tempted the woman, and the woman took the lead in taking the fruit and eating it, giving it to Adam who was with her. Adam was not the one deceived because the serpent wasn't speaking to him. Satan undermined God by speaking directly to the woman whom God gave as the only helper fit for the man. Satan went after the woman and attacked the most precious gift Adam had been given, the one whom he sang about:

> This at last is bone of my bones
>   and flesh of my flesh;
> she shall be called Woman,
>   because she was taken out of Man. (Gen. 2:23)

But God!

Yet she will be saved through [the] childbearing. I think what Paul is doing in his letter to Pastor Timothy is an appeal to the Ephesian women to repent of their disorderly conduct in corporate worship, and he appeals to them by recounting Eve's sin and sharing the same gospel promise that God gave to Eve in Genesis 3:15. So, according to this interpretation (which I recognize exists among other faithful interpretations of this text), if "she" in verse 15 is still talking about Eve, then the hope Eve has for salvation is in her offspring whom God promised would bruise the head of the serpent (Gen. 3:15)—the Lord Jesus Christ. We discussed previously in this book how Eve's first and second sons, Cain and Abel, turned out to decisively *not* be the hope she was looking for, and the promised Seed would come through her third son, Seth.

Every baby born after Seth would give the people hope that the Messiah was coming. Even now that our Messiah has come, we can be reminded of how God demonstrated his unparalleled faithfulness to keep his promises through sending his Son. This is good news! Since Eve was deceived and became a transgressor and yet would be saved through the promised offspring, who is Christ, then the Ephesian women were not hopeless in their sin, either. If the Ephesian women repent of their sin and continue in faith and love and holiness with self-control, then that would be very encouraging evidence of the Spirit's fruit in their lives, which would in turn comfort them that they were saved by grace through faith in Jesus. When we refuse to repent of our sin, we have no such comfort as this. I believe Paul was not tersely handing down angry rules to the Ephesian church ladies, but pastorally pointing them to the gospel and the encouraging assurance we have when we continue in faith, love, and holiness through the power of the Spirit.

Our Salvation Was Born of a Woman

And so, what about us? How will we consider this text in 1 Timothy 2 concerning God's design for leadership in his Son's body, the church? It is clear in the text, immediate context, and the whole of Scripture that we are not saved by birthing babies; so we need not act like we are (or imply that other women would be saved if they had kids). We can, therefore, reject out of hand any notion that women who give birth to children will be saved on the grounds of their childbearing and women who remain single or are childless are in eternal jeopardy. We can also see from the context that "through" in this verse is not a promise that every Christian woman will be saved (that is, her life preserved) through childbirth.

What we have here is a resounding, hope-full echo of the gospel by which we were saved—by grace through faith—in the finished work of Jesus on the cross. This is the trustworthy saying Paul refers to in the next verse (1 Tim. 3:1). All people everywhere who are delivered through the Redeemer who was "born of a woman" are recipients of God's undeserved, saving grace. What wondrous love! The fact that God saved men, women, and children from every tribe through his Son—the promised Seed, born of a woman—throws a blindingly brilliant spotlight on the dignity of motherhood. How we need this perspective as we live in cultures which alternatively denigrate and deify motherhood!

21

Children Are a Blessing

Unless the LORD builds the house,
    those who build it labor in vain.
Unless the LORD watches over the city,
    the watchman stays awake in vain.
It is in vain that you rise up early
    and go late to rest,
eating the bread of anxious toil;
    for he gives to his beloved sleep.
Behold, children are a heritage from the LORD,
    the fruit of the womb a reward.
Like arrows in the hand of a warrior
    are the children of one's youth.
Blessed is the man
    who fills his quiver with them!
He shall not be put to shame
    when he speaks with his enemies in the gate.

Psalm 127

Are you prepared for motherhood? On one hand, there really isn't a checklist of things you must be or accomplish in order to be adequately prepared for becoming a mother. But on the other hand, God equips his children for the ministries he has called them to, so your preparation is already on the way via his future grace. And still on another hand (how many hands are we on so far?), there are things expectant moms can do in order to prepare for the adventure of motherhood.

As you're expecting a child, you likely have a list of things you're working on. Perhaps you're stocking different sizes of diapers, learning about your adoptive child's medical needs, or reading about how to tell the difference between Braxton-Hicks contractions and "the real thing." Over the years, a few friends of mine have come over to be extra hands at my house before the births of their own babies, calling themselves "moms-in-training." (I've been praying for more friends who think this way!) As practically useful as all of our trainings can be, there is yet another training that will yield tremendous fruit in your life as a mom: feelings training.

Training Your Feelings

As we read and meditate on God's Word, our aim is to know our great God who loves us and called us to be his daughters by grace through faith in his Son. As we read the Bible, we inevitably come across things that are contrary to the way we feel. This is to be expected, though, because our feelings do not automatically line up with truth. But all is not lost; God has not left us without hope. We will be transformed by the renewal of our mind as we embrace and love and obey God's Word with the help of his Spirit. His Spirit also works in us as our powers of discernment are trained to recognize the truth and discern whether our feelings are in line with that truth.

When I say we need to train our feelings, what I mean is we need to train our feelings to submit to the truth revealed in God's Word. I'll be the first mom to raise my hand and say, "My feelings don't always correspond with the truth," and sometimes the way I deal with that is by rummaging around in the kitchen for some food to distract myself from the conflict I feel. Pretzel sticks in peanut butter help many things, but fixing my wayward feelings isn't one of them. We should ask God for help: "Help me, Father. My feelings don't match your Word. I want to love your Word and follow you more than I want to follow my feelings. Please change my feelings."

Some truths reveal our wayward feelings more often than others. For many people "children are a heritage from the LORD" is one of those truths that our emotions don't automatically, wholeheartedly affirm. One minute we joyfully embrace our heritage of children and the next minute we are on our knees begging God to increase our faith and trust him because our motherhood is so painful. It is so important for us to know that we do not have to rely on our feelings and emotions when we consider the children we raise. Contrary to the cultural opinions of our day, which are all over the map regarding how they view children, without any disclaimers, the Bible teaches that children are a heritage from the Lord. As God's humble creatures, we must look to him and his Word in order to understand what it means to be blessed.

As we've been learning throughout this book, God doesn't reflect us, but we are made in his image. And so on that note, we should know that the Bible teaches that God has a heritage. If your eyebrows just raised at that statement, then you've read it correctly. Yes, the Lord God who created everything you can see and cannot see and who rules over all things . . . has a heritage. He has something, or rather, *someones* whom he says are his heritage.

God's people—his saints—are his heritage. Everyone who is called out of the kingdom of darkness and born again by the Spirit is adopted into God's people. "Saints" he calls us, as he sees us through the righteousness of his crucified and resurrected Son.

Ask and I'll Give the Nations to You

One of the reasons our children are given as a heritage from the Lord is so that we can know and love our heavenly Father more and more. Our childbirth and fertility is not about us, but about God. He is not like us or made in our image, but we are like him, made in his image. As we saw in previous chapters, our feelings about motherhood and our multiplying of children are informed by what we believe about discipleship. Jesus's heritage is men, women, and children who are "put[ting] on the new self, which is being renewed in knowledge after the image of its Creator" (Col. 3:10). This fruitful multiplying (or "spiritual fertility") is the work of the Holy Spirit in and through us as we share the gospel and disciple people. Our feelings about fertility, birth, and motherhood are infused with gospel hope and an eternal perspective. Think of Paul—an unmarried man without biological children—who says he became Onesimus's spiritual father (Philem. 10)!

Our wayward feelings about motherhood—whether we are prone to glorying in it or growing bitter about it—need to consider the related truth that our Father has given his Son a heritage. What has Jesus inherited from his Father? His heritage, of course!

The Father's glorious inheritance in the saints—his children ransomed from death—he gives to his Son. Our family points us to God's family. These children whom Jesus suffered and died for are the joy that was set before him when he went to his crucifixion. They are the reward of his suffering. Because of them a new song of praise is being sung to Jesus:

Worthy are you to take the scroll
and to open its seals,
for you were slain, and by your blood you ransomed
people for God
from every tribe and language and people and nation,
and you have made them a kingdom and priests to
our God,
and they shall reign on the earth. (Rev. 5:9–10)

The writer of Hebrews says that Jesus is not ashamed to call us brothers: "Behold, I and the children God has given me" (Heb. 2:13). Here he is citing Isaiah 8:18, when just before a surprise Assyrian invasion the prophet Isaiah said, "Behold, I and the children whom the LORD has given me are signs and portents in Israel from the LORD of hosts, who dwells on Mount Zion." Will you, on the eve of battle, put all your trust in the Lord, who commands the armies of heaven? The "near" fulfillment of this prophetic word is that Isaiah and his children were physical signs among the people, attesting to the veracity of God's Word and the only reliable ally in the face of invasion. The "far" fulfillment of this prophetic word is that Jesus our Prophet, the Lord of hosts, stands together with the redeemed remnant—from every tribe and language and people and nation—awesome as an army with banners.

Christ's inheritance is the godly offspring given to him by his Father. "Behold, children are a heritage from the LORD, the fruit of the womb a reward" ultimately points us to Jesus, the Lord of hosts, the warrior whose quiver is full of arrows to be launched into a world that is dying without him. Jesus will not be put to shame as he builds his church, over which the gates of hell will not prevail.

Even though he was crushed by God and put to grief for our sins, Jesus was raised to eternal life and will see his offspring.

"Ask of me, and I will make the nations your heritage, and the ends of the earth your possession" (Ps. 2:8), his Father offered. The eternal Son of God asked, and he shall receive. Jesus is worthy to receive the reward of his suffering! And God's glorious Word is worthy of our trust even when our feelings disagree.

22

Knit Together

For you formed my inward parts;
    you knitted me together in my mother's womb.
I praise you, for I am fearfully and wonderfully made.
Wonderful are your works;
    my soul knows it very well.
My frame was not hidden from you,
when I was being made in secret,
    intricately woven in the depths of the earth.
Your eyes saw my unformed substance;
in your book were written, every one of them,
    the days that were formed for me,
    when as yet there was none of them.

Psalm 139:13–16

I remember we ate lunch in the food court: soft pretzels dipped in nacho cheese. Then we walked down the busy Toronto street to a pharmacy. I bought yet another pack of three home pregnancy tests (just to make sure). My husband and I returned to the hotel room where we were staying, and I took the test.

After an extremely long two-minute time period (which for some reason seemed much longer than the two-week period I waited to take the test), the two of us lifted the tissue to reveal the test results. Then we both burst into tears. After two years of negative tests, we were elated to see those two blue lines. After that day, time dragged on even more as we traveled to different training sessions for work. I couldn't wait to visit my doctor and get an ultrasound—I was desperate to see the baby. Eventually we did get to see her—our tiny daughter dancing on the ultrasound screen. Because I am a mom and this is part of my motherly duty, I regularly remind my middle schooler that even though she is as tall as me, she is always my baby girl.

Even before the hCG tests confirmed that I was pregnant with our daughter, her frame was not hidden from the Lord. She was being made in secret while her parents waited for confirmation. *I am fearfully and wonderfully made by God* is a tremendously encouraging thought. It is a summit too high for us to scale, a thought that sounds too good to be true. God's sovereignty over the details in our lives—from every thought we think to every word before we even utter it—is amazing. The writer of this psalm, King David, puts it this way,

> Such knowledge is too wonderful for me;
>> it is high; I cannot attain it. (Ps. 139:6)

And the Lord declares: "Who has made man's mouth? Who makes him mute, or deaf, or seeing, or blind? Is it not I, the Lord?" (Ex. 4:11).

The more I learn about the way God has designed the human body, the more I am amazed by God. This is the way it should be. As David implicitly teaches us through this psalm, our thoughts about our fearful and wonderful design should always, ever direct our hearts Godward. Babies sucking their thumbs on ultrasound are designed to direct our hearts to worship God. Those delicate swirls on your adoptive child's fingerprint on their passport paperwork are designed to direct your heart to worship God. What should you expect when you are expecting? Expect that God has designed every detail of your child's life to direct you (and them) to worship him.

Far Too Wonderful

God designed every detail of our lives to bring him praise. I can imagine varying responses to what I've just written. Your heart may be leaping with a joyous, "Yes, I agree!" Or your brow may be furrowed with a skeptical, "Um, wow?" Or you are already experiencing the foggy (but normal) "mommy brain" effect and cannot recall the words your eyes just passed over. (It's okay, friend! You can reread this paragraph one more time—you're in good company.) "I praise you, for I am fearfully and wonderfully made," David sings. We see God's handiwork, and we rejoice in him. Because God is perfect and everything he does is good, we can listen to this song on repeat—even in tears. His wisdom is far too wonderful for us to understand, but we praise him nonetheless.

Yes, we can praise God for his awesome creation even when we have questions; such praise is possible by grace through faith. There are so many times when we consider what God has designed and do not praise him for it. We might be self-absorbed, idolize our kids, or struggle with fear of man generally. We might openly criticize God and his design. Birth day timing, baby's health, baby's gender, our pregnancy conditions . . . we have so many desires we want to be fulfilled. But Psalm 139 teaches us that *the* fulfillment we are seeking is found only in God. It's part of the way he designed us!

Yes, Jesus Loves Us

We can praise God all the time, *even* when God has designed us with disabilities and ordained circumstances that are so difficult that it makes us weep. When Jesus's disciples inquired of him why a man was born blind (i.e., Did God *really* design this man this way?), his answer echoes this psalm: "That the works of God might be displayed in him" (John 9:1–3). It may not be now, but at some point in your life or your child's life, you will see something God has designed and be discouraged by it. God may not restore you or your child physically in this life, but by his grace he may restore and strengthen you spiritually through that pain. My own dear husband was exceptionally athletic throughout his youth, but when he turned twenty-eight, apart from a physical accident, his ulnar nerves stopped working properly and both of his arms became disabled. Living with this disability and chronic pain has been a tremendous trial for our family, but it is not apart from God's gracious design to satisfy us with himself as he brings himself glory. Every day we have practical reminders that we are weak and he is strong, and that yes, Jesus loves us! This is a greater treasure than healthy, pain-free bodies.

Because God is fearful and wonderful, everyone made in his image is fearfully and wonderfully made. Children are a blessing and a gift from God's hand. We've already discussed this, but it bears repeating now and every day: children are a blessing because they are from the Lord. Regardless of the packaging of the gift, the gift is precious because it is from God. Every child being made in secret by the Lord even at this moment is made—by his loving design—with some kind or degree of physical, emotional, mental, or developmental weaknesses. Some of these weaknesses don't manifest until later in life. Try as they may with their genetic technologies, scientists will never be able to engineer the "perfect, designer baby." The truth is that we are all so helpless and weak, and God is strong. The perspective on weakness and strength that honors God is the one that says, "I count everything as loss because of the surpassing worth of knowing Christ Jesus my Lord." Wouldn't we rather be weak vessels who consciously live by grace than be superlative specimens who don't know the Lord?

There's an expression that refers to time before a person was born as "before you were a twinkle in your daddy's eye." We've seen in Scripture that God has had each of us in mind from eternity past—having written in his book every day of our lives before we were born. Friend, this is a tremendously encouraging thought. God is pleased to be personally and intimately involved to knit together every individual human life in her mother's womb. In his own image he creates us. We are utterly dependent on God in every way, and he holds every minute of our lives in his capable, loving hands. From our conception to our resurrection, when Jesus will transform our lowly body to be like his glorious body, our response to God's exquisite handiwork is worship-full attitudes and expressive gratitude.

23

Don't Trust Birth; Trust God

In his hand is the life of every living thing
and the breath of all mankind.

Job 12:10

In that moment it didn't matter that I had studied childbirth, served as a doula, or already given birth to three children. I nodded off on the couch for a minute after I put our older kids to bed. Feeling horribly exhausted, I shuffled my thirty-eight-weeks pregnant self down the hallway. I took out my contact lenses, washed my face, sat down in the bathroom, and cried. My husband urged me to call the doctor to ask about medicine, and she told me to come see her in the morning. "Help me," I cried, so the doctor told me to call a taxi and meet her at the hospital. I hung up the phone and told my husband to call a babysitter and a taxi. Within a few minutes I was in shock, holding our newborn son in my arms. Needless to say, my husband called an ambulance instead of a taxi!

Diversity in the Hope Portfolio

We have many choices in which to place our hope—experts who are models of ingenuity, the illusion of human progress, nature and "her way," and even fatalism. The secular birthing admonition "Trust Birth" makes sense if there is no God. Who else can we trust? As cosmic orphans we're left to trust the systems we see at work in the world around us.

If our worldview is optimistic regarding "the way life is," then by faith we may trust that our bodies will work properly. Perhaps we admit that these things aren't perfect, but we don't presume that these systems will break on *us* in our hour of need. After all, we're smarter and stronger than our ancestors, and having babies simply isn't how it used to be . . . right?

Now, if there is a benevolent "god" out there somewhere but he is distant, then we must assess his character and his competency. We conclude that though he is no longer involved, this god did a good job in designing uteruses, hips, oxytocin, and umbilical cords. Therefore, any glitches we experience in childbirth are simply owing to our incomplete knowledge and application.

It's difficult for us to always know where exactly we've placed our hope. It is right to admire the amazing way our Creator God has designed our bodies to carry, birth, and nurture babies. Our admiration of creation should lead us to worship the Creator. For example, if we say we trust God while disregarding the common grace of sound medical treatment (a gift from God), it is not faith, but foolishness. Such a view comes from the abominable so-called prosperity gospel, not from wisdom. (For more information on this dangerous theology, please read the resources noted below.[1]) God has given us the remark-

---

1. See Sean DeMars, "The 'Gospel' That Almost Killed Me," the Gospel Coalition website, March 31, 2014, https://www.thegospelcoalition.org/article/the-gospel-that-almost-killed-me/; and *9Marks Journal*, "Prosperity Gospel: January–February 2014," 9Marks website, https://www.9marks.org/journal/prosperity-gospel/.

able privilege of stewarding his magnificent creation. One of the ways we steward God's creation is in caring for our bodies and faithfully using the gifts he's given us to do that extraordinary task. Prayerfully and carefully evaluating available medical care is faithful stewardship.

"Do Not Be Afraid." —Jesus

It matters where we place our hope because God is neither absent nor distant from us. He is not a back-up plan or a cheering birth coach. God defines reality. He is the sovereign God in whose hand is the life of every living thing and the breath of all mankind.

Waves of pain, floods of fear, and the slow-rising tide of impatience will invite us to trade our hope in God for anxiety or even self-induced naïveté about what's ahead. We need help to hope in God, accept gifts from his hands, and give him the thanks he is due. When anxious thoughts multiply within us, we direct them Godward (Ps. 94:19). The risen, ascended, and exalted Savior says, "Fear not, I am the first and the last, and the living one. I died, and behold I am alive forevermore, and I have the keys of Death and Hades" (Rev. 1:17–18). It is this God in whom we place our trust to save us from our sin and never leave us or forsake us. *All of our trust.*

Who answers prayer? Birth? No, the Lord answers prayer.

> Hear my prayer, O LORD;
> let my cry come to you!
> Do not hide your face from me
>   in the day of my distress!
> Incline your ear to me;
>   answer me speedily in the day when I call! (Ps. 102:1–2)

Who is the rock and fortress? The birthing mother? No, it is the Lord who made her and loves her.

> I love you, O LORD, my strength.
> The LORD is my rock and my fortress and my deliverer,
>   my God, my rock, in whom I take refuge,
>   my shield, and the horn of my salvation, my
>   stronghold. (Ps. 18:1–2)

As we saw in the previous chapter, God's wisdom is displayed in how he designed our bodies. And as we saw in the first half of this book, our sin has broken everything, including our bodies. Lest we stop short here and declare that apart from our sin we are free to trust in birth, we recall how Eve lived in perfect dependence on God before the fall. In our admiration of how God designed women's bodies we do not assume that Eve in her pre-fall, physically perfect body would have trusted her body in lieu of her Creator. Before Adam and Eve sinned, they perfectly trusted God—at all times and without reservation.

Now, post-fall, in our experience of childbirth we echo Eve's cry of praise to the Lord when she gave birth outside the garden of Eden in the wilderness: "I have gotten a man with the help of the LORD" (Gen. 4:1). *Lest the reader misunderstand, even while we are wise to hire doctors, take childbirth classes, use pain medicine, hire a birth coach, or employ any other helpful means for safe and comfortable childbirth, we see these gifts as from God's hand.* Praise him for his grace and help! It is the Lord himself who is our refuge in life and death. And that is the happiest and highest thought one can have.

24

God Who Causes to Bring Forth

"Before she was in labor
　　she gave birth;
before her pain came upon her
　　she delivered a son.
Who has heard such a thing?
　　Who has seen such things?
Shall a land be born in one day?
　　Shall a nation be brought forth in one moment?
For as soon as Zion was in labor
　　she brought forth her children.
Shall I bring to the point of birth and not cause to bring
　　　forth?"
　　says the LORD;
"shall I, who cause to bring forth, shut the womb?"
　　says your God.

Isaiah 66:7–9

As the time draws nearer to the birth of your child, you may be weighing your options regarding childbirth. If you live in a context where you have many choices available to you, this topic might be overwhelming. Certain resources and interventions might be considered necessary/unnecessary, preferred/avoided, available/unaccessible, effective/ineffective, culturally acceptable/taboo, safe/dangerous, affordable/cost-prohibitive, negligible/significant, and so on. It may be that divisive controversies and opinions swirl around childbirth in your community. Our cultures, beliefs, personal experiences, and economic status play no small part in forming our perspective on such things. If you live in a place where technologies and resources are readily available to give comfort and pain relief to birthing mothers, then praise God for the gifts that come from his hand.

With all that being said, I think it is safe to say that when push comes to shove (pun intended) and a laboring mother is beyond exhausted so much so that she and her baby are in jeopardy, life-saving intervention is in order. The labor room pulses with energy while supportive voices chant "Push!" and medical professionals consider a host of intervening means of delivering mom and baby.

It is remarkable how Scripture uses this scenario—when children come to the point of birth and there is no strength to bring them forth—to describe our helplessness to save ourselves and God's ability to deliver us.

A Labor without Hope

In order to fully appreciate our text above from Isaiah 66, we need to see that Israel knew she couldn't do it—she could not save herself.

> Like a pregnant woman
>> who writhes and cries out in her pangs
>> when she is near to giving birth,

so were we because of you, O LORD;
    we were pregnant, we writhed,
    but we have given birth to wind.
We have accomplished no deliverance in the earth,
    and the inhabitants of the world have not fallen.
      (Isa. 26:17–18)

It was the word on the street. Everyone knew their efforts were just giving birth to wind. For all of their writhing, the people knew they couldn't deliver themselves because of their sin. Just beyond the gates of Jerusalem, the Assyrian army stood ready to devour them. All the way in the palace the king felt the weight of their situation, and he couldn't save them either: "They said to [Isaiah], 'Thus says [King] Hezekiah, "This day is a day of distress, of rebuke, and of disgrace; children have come to the point of birth, and there is no strength to bring them forth"'" (Isa. 37:3).

Distress, rebuke, disgrace. Theirs was a labor that could not accomplish salvation—a labor without hope. *But God!* He made a promise. "For I will defend this city to save it, for my own sake and for the sake of my servant David" (Isa. 37:35). In his mercy God would cause the tribe of Judah to survive so that Zion would deliver a son—the Son—and bring forth children. Yahweh would fulfill his promise that the Messiah he promised would come through the seed of the woman.

Who Has Ever Heard of Such a Thing as *Grace*?

"Grace? Is this a name?" Depending on your context, you may be surprised to learn that the Christian concept of grace is foreign to the world. Many of my friends either do not know of or do not commonly use a word for *grace* in their mother tongues. Even those of us who grew up with a Christian worldview struggle with grace. "Surely there's something I have to *do*," our dubious hearts wonder.

God's work in salvation is beyond any intervention mankind could ever conceive. The grace of God given to us in the crucified and risen Jesus Christ will forever be the greatest gift of love in history. You cannot earn this love or repay him for it. Our God is a God of grace. "Before she was in labor she gave birth; before her pain came upon her she delivered a son." A *prelabor* birth? Who has heard of such a thing as . . . grace?

What Zion could not do for herself, Yahweh would do for her and all who put their trust in him. Just like when God overcame Sarah's barrenness and gave her Isaac, God would overcome Israel's barrenness, also. God alone would cause the Messiah to be brought forth out of the tribe of Judah. God alone is the one who would cause his holy nation from every tribe, tongue, and people group to be brought forth in one moment. God alone would fulfill his promise to Abraham that through his offspring all the world would be blessed. God and God alone is in control and orchestrates all things—shall he bring to the point of birth and not bring forth?

Nothing Compares to the Cross

Throughout the history of redemption, God worked on behalf of his people. He gave birth to Israel, redeeming them from Egypt and experiencing birth pain at the rock of Meribah (Ex. 17:1–7; Deut. 32:18). He promised an even greater new creation work through the Servant, once again experiencing birth pain (Isa. 42:14).

All of this points to the cross. Jesus willingly gave his life as our substitute—he became sin for us and bore the wrath of God. What is the result of his unprecedented, incomparably fruitful labor? God has accomplished nothing less than the birth of a new humanity through the judgment borne by his Servant on the cross. A new humanity born without biological labor—

this is our spiritual adoption. You and I can be adopted children of Yahweh because of the cross. It is the intervention of all interventions. Do you like to hear birth stories? Well, talk about a labor that is unlike anyone has ever seen or heard . . . ever!

We're not biologically born into God's family; we're spiritually adopted, labored over by Yahweh himself, and born again without birth pain. "'Sing, O barren woman, who did not bear; break forth into singing and cry aloud, you who have not been in labor! For the children of the desolate one will be more than the children of her who is married,' says the LORD" (Isa. 54:1). Jesus accomplished for Israel what they could not do for themselves. The curse of birth pain is reversed through the cross, where Jesus accomplishes salvation and begets new covenant children who far exceed the biological children of ethnic Israel.

Turn to Me and Be Saved

Some have argued, "Jesus could not have reversed the curse because there is still birth pain." But Jesus declared, "I am the resurrection and the life. Whoever believes in me, *though he die*, yet shall he live" (John 11:25). All over the world mothers undergo birth pain, but for those who believe in Jesus, even if their birth pain leads to death, they will be resurrected to eternal life. Others have argued that our text in Isaiah 66 is a "name it and claim it" promise that your upcoming childbirth will be painless if you have faith. That is a gross misinterpretation of the text, as you can see from the biblical theology of birth pain. We do not expect painless childbearing, but we do expect grace upon grace in our painful childbearing. The Bible doesn't say that your life will not involve "tribulation, or distress, or persecution, or famine, or nakedness, or danger, or sword" (Rom. 8:31–35). It may be that one of those terrible things eventually separates you from earthly comfort or earthly life, but *nothing* will ever, ever separate you from the love of Christ.

In all occasions, then, and not only in our childbearing, do we find hope and comfort in Christ alone. As ever, rest and boast in God's power as the time which God appointed for childbirth or for your child's homecoming approaches. And to my friends who feel they are far off from God, today would you consider the wondrous grace of God? He who bore the judgment for your sin says to you, "Turn to me and be saved, all ends of the earth! For I am God, and there is no other" (Isa. 45:22).

This grace is available for all. Yahweh announces his good news for all people that "by his knowledge shall the righteous one, my servant, make many to be accounted righteous, and he shall bear their iniquities" (Isa. 53:11). Salvation by grace through faith is an intervention that reaches beyond socio-economic status, cultural preferences, and personalities. God, being rich in mercy, because of the great love with which he loved us, even when we were dead in our trespasses, made us alive together with Christ—by grace we have been saved!

25

From Inevitable Sorrow
to Guaranteed Joy

Truly, truly, I say to you, you will weep and lament, but the world will rejoice. You will be sorrowful, but your sorrow will turn into joy. When a woman is giving birth, she has sorrow because her hour has come, but when she has delivered the baby, she no longer remembers the anguish, for joy that a human being has been born into the world. So also you have sorrow now, but I will see you again, and your hearts will rejoice, and no one will take your joy from you.

John 16:20–22

Layla is twenty weeks pregnant—she has several more months to wait. In the meantime, she is experiencing what her doctors consider to be a normal, healthy pregnancy. "Everything is fine," they assure her, and yet my friend lives with a nagging fear that something . . . *any*thing . . . could go awry at any moment. She feels the baby kick, hears stories, watches videos, and reads articles, and then she builds imaginary scenarios in her mind that haunt her dreams and steal her joy. Conversations with Layla always circle back to her fear of the "what if?"

"I can't be happy until I know *for sure* everything is going to be okay," she says. My friend struggles to see how the anguish she is experiencing can give way to joy.

Can you relate? I sure can. All of us, like my friend Layla, need assurance. We need *real* hope. We live in a world where we "do not know what tomorrow will bring." We live with unrelenting reminders that teach us to ask ourselves, "What is your life? For you are a mist that appears for a little time and then vanishes" (James 4:14). So, then, what should we do? Let the fear of "what if?" become our god and make sacrifices to it? Bow down to our rational fears, hand over our joy, and live according to what our fears dictate?

Nine Months Is a Mist

It's fascinating that Jesus told his disciples (a group of men who did not personally experience the anguish of knowing their hour had come to give birth) to see this tangible, intimate, intense scene of a birthing mother as an illustration of their current sorrow and guaranteed joy. The illustration Jesus gives is clear: the mother forgets her anguish because she is holding her baby—who was more than worth the wait and the suffering it took to bring him into this world. Whether or not you or I (or any disciple of Jesus) ever experience birth pain is not the point. Whether or not you or I suffer to bring children into this world is also not the point. Jesus doesn't minimize the pain of childbirth, either; he highlights the incomparable joy that is the outcome. In the face of all our sorrow-inducing fears, our hearts are assured that Christ has conquered death and guaranteed our everlasting joy. Our anguish will give way to joy because Jesus has gone before us and conquered death.

What do you do when all of your imagined "what if?" fears . . . and any actual, presented fears . . . take your breath away? When we tremble in our beds awake at night, we thank God for the opportunity to number our days and fear him. We take captive every thought to the obedience of Christ (2 Cor. 10:5), and we fill our minds with what is true, honorable, just, pure, lovely, commendable, excellent, and worthy of praise (Phil. 4:8). We repent of all the ways we demand to be in control of the universe, and we rest in our heavenly Father's care.

We remember what Jesus said to his disciples on the night he was betrayed, just before he was led away by a cohort of soldiers: "You will see me again." This promise still rang true as Jesus was tried in kangaroo court after kangaroo court and sentenced to death. "You will see me again." As he hung on the cross, crucified for our sin to satisfy the wrath of God, it was still true. "You will see me again." His body—wrapped in swaddling clothes and laid in a manger at his birth, was wrapped in grave clothes and laid in a borrowed tomb at his death. Even then, "You will see me again." A group of women went together to see him again at his tomb, but they went with burial spices. They were still weeping and lamenting. But instead of working to prepare the Lord Jesus's dead body for burial, they met the risen Savior whose finished work on the cross made them part of his new creation. His disciples did see him again, along with hundreds of other eye-witnesses. The rest of us, for two millennia, have also seen him. We see Jesus through the work of his Spirit in the lives of saints who have joined the cloud of witnesses before us and in the lives of believers who labor with hope among us.

Friend, if your waiting time feels like forever, or it feels like terror, or it feels like you're on a rocking chair spending all this energy to go nowhere, set your hope on Christ. Whether your anxiety is growing as you watch your belly grow or you watch the complications of the adoption process grow, Christ is willing and able to give you his peace.

The Fragrance of Our Expectancy

As we wait we also thank God, who in Christ always leads us in triumphal procession like the way a conquering general leads his soldiers in the victory parade. (It's a good thing the spiritual armor of God [Eph. 6:10–20] fits over maternity elastic!)

Wherever God sends us, the fragrance of the knowledge of Christ wafts through the world. It's a very different smell depending on who you are. Your labor with hope in a world of sorrow smells like death to one person, but life to another. God's work is not like ours; our work is like God's. God works in you as you make sacrifices to raise the children he gives you, and he works in the people around you as they smell the aroma of Christ in your presence.

Followers of Christ have sorrow while the world revels in its rejection of the Savior. Their fears are temporal and mist-like when compared to God's eternal judgment for sin. When I asked my friend Azar if she was afraid to talk about Jesus with her family (who could legally hand her over for imprisonment for being a Christian), she said, "I've been rescued from the worst thing that could ever happen to me when I was apart from Jesus. What can they do to me that is worse than that?" Layla needs to know and you and I need to know that there is no earthly fear—real or imagined—that is worse than perishing apart from Jesus. And we need to know the corresponding truth that there is no joy we can have right now—real or imagined—

that can surpass the joy of knowing Jesus in this life and the power of his resurrection.

We have seen in Scripture that fertility, pregnancy, birth, and birth pain are pointers to the one for whom we were made and all things exist. In all these things we look not to ourselves, but to Christ alone. The Bible teaches us to understand our childbearing and pain in relation to the eschatological rumbling of this age that will culminate in the new creation. A mother forgets the anguish it cost her to bring the baby home or to birth the baby because she is holding her child—her joy. The expectant hope we have is that our resurrection glory will far outweigh any grief we experience as we follow Christ. Through our maternal labors God is teaching us to glorify him in all things and join the deafening, thunderous applause of heaven when the saints fall prostrate before the Lamb to whom belongs all glory, power, dominion, and authority.

Press on, sister, as you follow Jesus into all of the maternal labors ahead of you. Who is sufficient for these things? Christ is, and the day is coming quickly when we will wait for Jesus's return no longer. The anguish will be forgotten when our faith becomes sight. We know for sure that everything is going to be *far more than* okay. We will see him again. In the meantime, no one can take away our joy. Ever.

> For from him and through him and to him are all things.
> To him be glory forever. Amen.
>
> Romans 11:36

Scripture Index